VOCA EDGE

KB234030

Level 6

We're

Introduction

Every student knows acquiring English vocabulary is a basic necessity for learning the English language. However, not many are aware that simply memorizing vocabulary words is not enough. In order to master a language, students need to spend more time learning how to use these words and what they really mean. Yet, students still spend countless hours memorizing rather than learning.

Even worse is the fact that most vocabulary books are extremely difficult and boring. Fortunately, there is a way for everyone to change their perspective on learning vocabulary. Now you can develop your vocabulary in an enjoyable way. The VOCA EDGE SMART series will help you simultaneously enlarge your vocabulary and improve your English.

This series uses an integrated approach to learning English. Listening, reading, writing and comprehension are all covered in this series.

One of the key features of this series is that it revolves around the daily lives of several characters and the challenges they face in growing up. By reading each episode, students will learn the natural and functional use of English vocabulary.

Each level of this series comes with one textbook and one audio component. Each book is organized into 6 chapters, each of which consists of 2-4 related units. Each book also deals with a variety of unique and interesting topics, and the series is graded to an appropriate length and depth to suit the needs of students with varying levels of English proficiency.

After studying each unit, students will be challenged to review the words and expressions they learned through a series of related questions and activities. Students can listen to the entire script in MP3 format. We invite you to let this series help you take the next step in your journey towards becoming a more proficient speaker of English. We are confident that the VOCA EDGE SMART series can help you make a dramatic improvement in your English ability.

Contents

책의 구성과 특징

1단계

- Preview 단계로, 주어진 삽화를 보고 각 Unit의 에피소드를 먼저 추측해볼 수 있습니다.

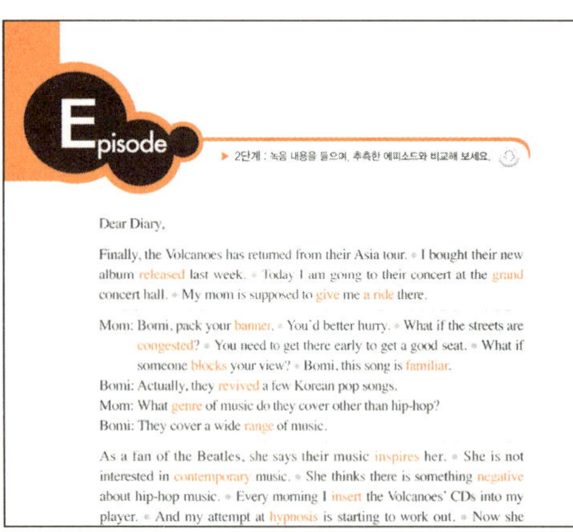

2단계

- 일기, 대화, 편지 등의 다양한 형태로 제공된 10대의 일상 생활 속 에피소드를 눈으로 읽고 귀로 듣는 단계로, 어휘뿐만 아니라 Reading 및 Listening, Conversation 학습 효과까지 누릴 수 있습니다.

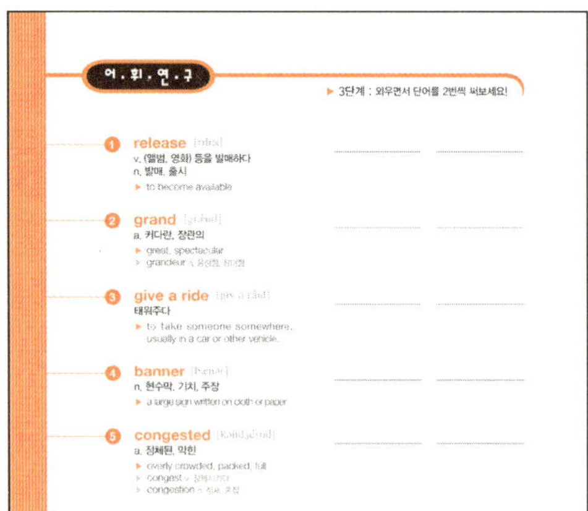

3단계

- 앞의 지문에서 가장 중요한 어휘만을 골라 익히고 연습하는 단계로, 각 단어와 관련된 유의어 및 반의어, 파생어를 함께 학습할 수 있습니다.

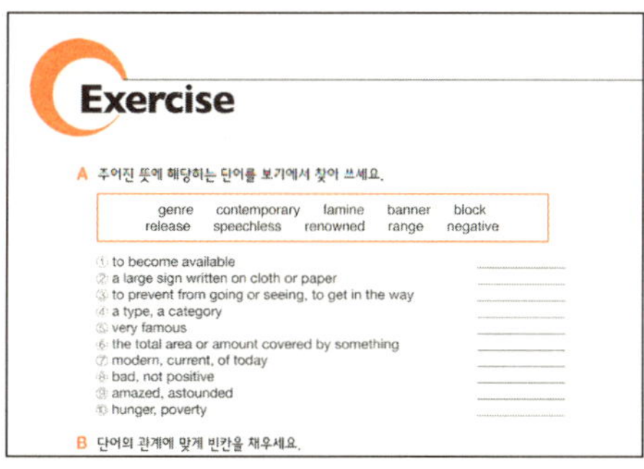

Exercise

- 중요한 단어 및 표현들을 빈칸에 채워 넣으며, 앞에서 배운 어휘들을 다시 확인하고 점검할 수 있습니다.

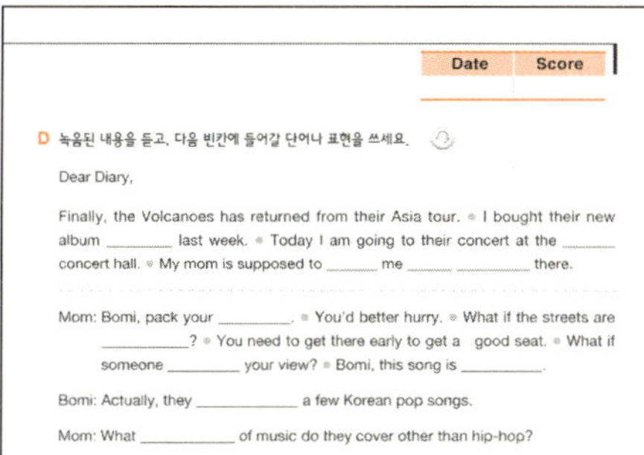

Dictation

- CD를 듣고 빈칸에 해당하는 단어를 채워 넣으며, Unit의 전체 내용을 복습할 수 있습니다. 또한, 자신의 약점을 파악하여 취약부분만을 집중적으로 학습할 수 있습니다.

Review Test

- 각 챕터가 끝나면 앞에서 배운 중요한 단어 30개를 듣고 받아씀으로써, 정확한 발음 공부와 함께 단어 복습도 함께 할 수 있습니다.

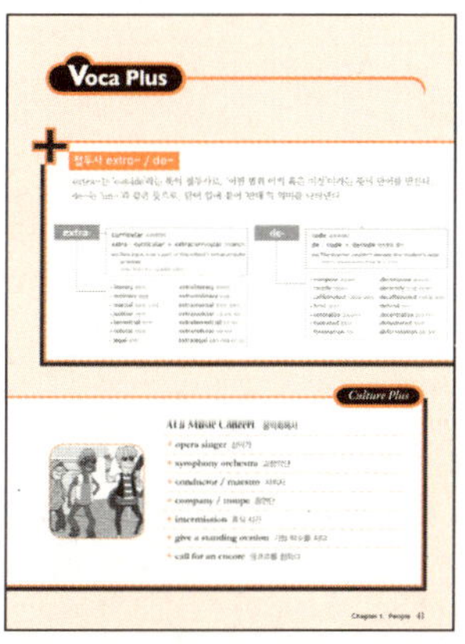

Voca Plus

- 영단어들이 어떻게 구성되어 있는지에 대해 어원을 포함한 기본적인 정보들을 배우며, 각 챕터와 관련된 문화 정보와 필수 어휘들도 함께 익힐 수 있습니다.

SMART **L**evel.6

VOCA EDGE

Chapter 1 — People

Chapter 1 People

▶ 1단계 : 먼저 그림을 보고, 이 장의 에피소드를 추측해 보세요.

→ have fame all over the world

make an attempt at hypnosis ←

→ become more receptive

Dear Diary,

Finally, the Volcanoes has returned from their Asia tour. ● I bought their new album released last week. ● Today I am going to their concert at the grand concert hall. ● My mom is supposed to give me a ride there.

Mom: Bomi, pack your banner. ● You'd better hurry. ● What if the streets are congested? ● You need to get there early to get a good seat. ● What if someone blocks your view? ● Bomi, this song is familiar.
Bomi: Actually, they revived a few Korean pop songs.
Mom: What genre of music do they cover other than hip-hop?
Bomi: They cover a wide range of music.

As a fan of the Beatles, she says their music inspires her. ● She is not interested in contemporary music. ● She thinks there is something negative about hip-hop music. ● Every morning I insert the Volcanoes' CDs into my player. ● And my attempt at hypnosis is starting to work out. ● Now she seems to be becoming more receptive to their music. ● She knows that there are many Volcanoes' fanatics all over the world. ● Now she knows that they have fame all over the world. ● She also knows that they are renowned even in Japan.

I always tell my mom that my hero, Youngwoong, attracts people like a magnet. ● Youngwoong is passionate about music. ● He always says, "Music sustains me." ● Doesn't he sound like a specialist? ● If mom saw him playing the electric guitar, she would be speechless. ● Today's concert is meaningful. ● The profit is going to be used to help the kids with leukemia. ● It will also be used to help the kids suffering from famine.

▶ 3단계 : 외우면서 단어를 2번씩 써보세요!

1 release [rilíːs]
v. (앨범, 영화) 등을 발매하다
n. 발매, 출시
▶ to become available

2 grand [grǽnd]
a. 커다란, 장관의
▶ great, spectacular
▷ grandeur n. 웅장함, 장대함

3 give a ride [gív ə ràid]
태워주다
▶ to take someone somewhere, usually in a car or other vehicle.

4 banner [bǽnər]
n. 현수막, 기치, 주장
▶ a large sign written on cloth or paper

5 congested [kəndʒéstid]
a. 정체된, 막힌
▶ overly crowded, packed, full
▷ congest v. 정체시키다
▷ congestion n. 정체, 혼잡

6 block [blɑk]
v. 막다, 차단하다
n. 블록
▶ to prevent from going or seeing, to get in the way

7 familiar [fəmíljər]
a. 익숙한, 친숙한
▶ well acquainted, well-known
▷ familiarize v. 친숙하게 하다
▷ familiarity n. 친함, 잘 앎

▶ 외우면서 단어를 2번씩 써보세요!

8 revive [riváiv]
v. 되살리다, 재공연하다
▶ to bring back to life; to present a new production of a song, a play, or an opera
▶ revival n. 부활, 재생, 리바이벌

9 genre [ʒá:nrə]
n. 장르
▶ a type, a category

10 range [reindʒ]
n. 범주, 범위
▶ the total area or amount covered by something

11 inspire [inspáiər]
v. 영감을 주다, 고무시키다
▶ to influence someone to do something in a positive way
▶ inspiration n. 영감
▶ inspirational a. 고무적인, 영감을 주는

12 contemporary [kəntémpərèri]
a. 동시대의, 현대의
▶ modern, current, of today

13 negative [négətiv]
a. 부정적인
▶ bad, not positive

14 insert [insə́:rt]
v. 넣다, 삽입하다
▶ to put something into something else
▶ insertion n. 삽입, 끼워넣음

▶ 3단계 : 외우면서 단어를 2번씩 써보세요!

15 hypnosis [hipnóusis]
n. 최면
▶ a form of mind control
▶ hypnotize v. 최면을 걸다
▶ hypnotism n. 최면술, 최면상태

16 receptive [riséptiv]
a. 수용적인, 받아들이는
▶ open and responsive to ideas
▶ reception n. 수용

17 fanatic [fənǽtik]
n. 열광자, 광신자
▶ a person who is crazy or who has a strong interest in something
▶ fanatical a. 광적인, 열중한

18 fame [feim]
n. 명성
▶ a measure of being famous, renown
▶ famous a. 유명한

19 renowned [rináund]
a. 유명한
▶ very famous
▶ renown n. 명성

20 magnet [mǽgnit]
n. 자석
▶ something that attracts or draws other things
▶ magnetic a. 자석의

21 passionate [pǽʃənit]
a. 열정적인
▶ capable of expressing intense feeling or caring greatly
▶ passion n. 열정

▶ 외우면서 단어를 2번씩 써보세요!

22 sustain [səstéin]

v. 지탱하다, 기운내게 하다

▶ to keep alive, to support
▷ sustenance n. 지탱, 유지
▷ sustainable a. 지탱할 수 있는

23 specialist [spéʃəlist]

n. 전문가

▶ a person who is extremely skilled in a particular thing
▷ specialize v. 전문으로 하다

24 electric [iléktrik]

a. 전기의

▶ powered by electricity
▷ electricity n. 전기
▷ electrical a. 전기에 관한

25 speechless [spìːtʃlis]

a. 감탄한, 말문이 막힐 정도로 놀란

▶ amazed, astounded

26 meaningful [míːniŋfəl]

a. 의미 있는

▶ having a purpose or reason

27 leukemia [luːkíːmiə]

n. 백혈병

▶ a deadly form of cancer (characterized by an abnormal increase in the number of white blood cells in one's body)

28 famine [fǽmin]

n. 기아

▶ hunger, poverty

Exercise

A 주어진 뜻에 해당하는 단어를 보기에서 찾아 쓰세요.

> genre　　contemporary　　famine　　banner　　block
> release　　speechless　　renowned　　range　　negative

① to become available ＿＿＿＿＿＿＿
② a large sign written on cloth or paper ＿＿＿＿＿＿＿
③ to prevent from going or seeing, to get in the way ＿＿＿＿＿＿＿
④ a type, a category ＿＿＿＿＿＿＿
⑤ very famous ＿＿＿＿＿＿＿
⑥ the total area or amount covered by something ＿＿＿＿＿＿＿
⑦ modern, current, of today ＿＿＿＿＿＿＿
⑧ bad, not positive ＿＿＿＿＿＿＿
⑨ amazed, astounded ＿＿＿＿＿＿＿
⑩ hunger, poverty ＿＿＿＿＿＿＿

B 단어의 관계에 맞게 빈칸을 채우세요.

① magnet : ＿＿＿＿＿＿＿＿ = 자석 : 자석의
② fame : famous = 명성 : ＿＿＿＿＿＿＿＿
③ insert : ＿＿＿＿＿＿＿＿ = 삽입하다 : 삽입
④ grand : ＿＿＿＿＿＿＿＿ = 커다란 : 웅장한
⑤ ＿＿＿＿＿＿＿＿ : congest = 정체된 : 정체시키다
⑥ revive : ＿＿＿＿＿＿＿＿ = 되살리다 : 부활
⑦ inspire : inspiration = 고무시키다 : ＿＿＿＿＿＿＿＿
⑧ hypnosis : hypnotism = 최면 : ＿＿＿＿＿＿＿＿

C 의미가 같도록 알맞은 단어를 넣어 문장을 완성하세요.

1. It will also be used to help the kids suffering from ＿＿＿＿＿＿＿ .
그것은 또한 기아로 고통 받는 아이들을 돕는 데에도 쓰일 거야.

2. Today's concert is ＿＿＿＿＿＿＿ .
오늘의 콘서트는 의미 있어.

3. If mom saw him playing the ＿＿＿＿＿＿＿ guitar, she would be speechless.
만일 엄마가 그가 전자기타 연주하는 모습을 보신다면, 감탄하실 거야.

4. Doesn't he sound like a ＿＿＿＿＿＿＿ ?
정말 전문가다운 소리 아닌가?

5. He always says, "Music ＿＿＿＿＿＿＿ me."
그는 늘 "음악이 나를 지탱한다"라고 말해.

6. Youngwoong is ＿＿＿＿＿＿＿ about music.
그는 음악에 열정적이야.

7. She knows that there are many Volcanoes' ＿＿＿＿＿＿＿ all over the world.
그녀는 전 세계적으로 볼케이노의 열혈팬들이 많다는 것을 알고 계셔.

8. Now she seems to be becoming more ＿＿＿＿＿＿＿ to their music.
이제 그녀는 그들의 음악을 좀 더 받아들이기 시작하는 것 같아.

D 녹음된 내용을 듣고, 다음 빈칸에 들어갈 단어나 표현을 쓰세요.

Dear Diary,

Finally, the Volcanoes has returned from their Asia tour. ● I bought their new album _________ last week. ● Today I am going to their concert at the _______ concert hall. ● My mom is supposed to _______ me _____ _________ there.

Mom: Bomi, pack your __________. ● You'd better hurry. ● What if the streets are ____________? ● You need to get there early to get a   good seat. ● What if someone __________ your view? ● Bomi, this song is ___________.

Bomi: Actually, they _____________ a few Korean pop songs.

Mom: What ____________ of music do they cover other than hip-hop?

Bomi: They cover a wide _______________ of music.

As a fan of the Beatles, she says their music _________ her. ● She is not interested in _____________ music. ● She thinks there is something _________ about hip-hop music. ● Every morning I ________ the Volcanoes' CDs into my player. ● And my attempt at _________ is starting to work out. ● Now she seems to be becoming more _________ to their music. ● She knows that there are many Volcanoes' _________ all over the world. ● Now she knows that they have ________ all over the world. ● She also knows that they are __________ even in Japan.

I always tell my mom that my hero, Youngwoong, attracts people like a _________. ● Youngwoong is __________ about music. ● He always says, "Music _________ me." ● Doesn't he sound like a _____________? ● If mom saw him playing the _________ guitar, she would be __________. ●Today's concert is __________. ● The profit is going to be used to help the kids with _________. ● It will also be used to help the kids suffering from ___________. ●

Chapter 1 People

→ **make a strenuous effort**

know the fundamental principles ←

→ **advocate a halt to the war**

Dear Sara,

What induced Hoony to change like that? ● He has been subscribing to a science magazine. ● He even read the biography of Albert Einstein. ● He thinks it is important to know the fundamental principles of physics. ● Today he showed me a strange formula. ● Itwas Einstein's theory of relativity. ● Hoony wants to be the first Korean physicist to win the Nobel Prize. ● He's becoming very patriotic. ● He is also making a strenuous effort to improve his water rocket. ● He spends entirely too much time experimenting with his rocket. ● Then he puts it on the shelf to keep it intact. ● He polishes it with wax every morning.

Bomi: Why are you pasting the metal pieces on its body?
Hoony: I'm trying to make my rocket fly for the longest period of time. ● I
　　　will make this extraordinary. ● Finally, it will surpass Minsu's.

Sara, does your brother still enjoy making presidential speeches? ● I hope he gets elected school president, competing with 5 other candidates. ● Once he makes his pledges to do well in front of the students, they will vote for him. ● He will attain his goal of being elected. ● I remember him being quite an eloquent speaker. ● He demonstrated his abilities in front of the American Embassy. ● At that time he was advocating a halt to the war. ● He tried to emphasize non-violence. ● I'm sure your brother will be a good statesman.

▶ 3단계 : 외우면서 단어를 2번씩 써보세요!

1 induce [indjúːs]
v. 유도하다, 권유하다
▶ to cause to happen
▶ inducement n. 유도, 권유

2 subscribe [səbskráib]
v. 정기구독하다
▶ to sign up in order to receive something periodically
▶ subscription n. 정기구독
▶ subscribe to ~을 정기구독하다

3 biography [baiɑ̀grəfi]
n. 전기
▶ a book written about a person
▶ autobiography n. 자서전
▶ biographical a. 전기적인, 전기문의

4 fundamental [fʌ̀ndəméntl]
a. 근본적인
▶ of central importance
▶ fundamentally ad. 근본적으로

5 formula [fɔ́ːrmjələ]
n. 공식
▶ a set of numbers and characters expressing a scientific rule

6 relativity [rèlətívəti]
n. 상대성
▶ a scientific law discovered by Einstein that is fundamental to physics
▶ relative a. 상대적인
▶ relatively ad. 상대적으로

7 physicist [fízisist]
n. 물리학자
▶ a person who studies and researches the science of physics
▶ physics n. 물리학

▶ 외우면서 단어를 2번씩 써보세요!

8 patriotic [pèitriátik]
a. 애국심이 강한, 애국적인
▶ strongly supporting one's own country
▶ patriot n. 애국자
▶ patriotism n. 애국심

9 strenuous [strénjuəs]
a. 부단한, 분투를 요하는
▶ demanding or requiring vigorous exertion, laborious

10 entirely [entáiərli]
ad. 아주, 전적으로
▶ completely, absolutely
▶ entire a. 전적인

11 intact [intǽkt]
a. 손상되지 않은, 손대지 않은
▶ undamaged, uninjured

12 polish [páliʃ]
v. 광을 내다
▶ to rub something to make it shiny
▶ polished a. 광을 낸

13 metal [métl]
n. 금속
▶ a hard substance such as iron and steel

14 period [píəriəd]
n. 기간
▶ the amount of time between two points
▶ periodical n. 정기간행물
▶ periodic a. 주기적인

▶ 3단계 : 외우면서 단어를 2번씩 써보세요!

15 extraordinary [ikstrɔ́ːrdənèri]
a. 비범한, 우수한
▶ exceptional, marvelous
▶ extraordinarily ad. 비범하게, 특별히

16 surpass [sərpǽs]
v. 능가하다
▶ to outdo someone or something

17 presidential [prèzidénʃəl]
a. 회장의, 대통령의
▶ having to do with the president
▶ president n. 회장, 대통령

18 elect [ilékt]
v. 선출하다
▶ to choose someone by voting for them
▶ election n. 선출, 선거

19 candidate [kǽndədèit]
n. 후보자
▶ a person attempting to be hired, elected, etc. for a position

20 pledge [pledʒ]
n. 공약, 서약
v. 서약하다, 공약하다
▶ a promise to do something
▶ make a pledge 공약하다

21 attain [ətéin]
v. 달성하다
▶ to achieve something, to accomplish
▶ attainment n. 달성, 성취
▶ attainable a. 성취할 수 있는

▶ 외우면서 단어를 2번씩 써보세요!

22 eloquent [éləkwənt]

a. 말재주 있는, 웅변의
- ▶ very well-spoken and well-mannered
- ▶ eloquence n. 웅변, 호소력
- ▶ eloquently ad. 호소력 있게, 웅변력 있게

23 embassy [émbəsi]

n. 대사관
- ▶ the official residence and office of an ambassador

24 advocate [ǽdvəkit]

v. 주장하다, 옹호하다
- ▶ to recommend a particular action or plan publicly

25 halt [hɔːlt]

n. 정지 v. 멈추다
- ▶ the end, stoppage

26 non-violence [nɑn váiələns]

n. 비폭력
- ▶ abstention from violence, nonaggression
- ▶ non-violent a. 비폭력의

27 statesman [stéitsmən]

n. 정치인
- ▶ a politician; a person well-educated in politics and government

Exercise

A 주어진 뜻에 해당하는 단어를 보기에서 찾아 쓰세요.

> halt   intact   candidate   embassy   statesman
> advocate   pledge   surpass   extraordinary   metal

① a politician; a person well-educated in politics and government __________
② the end, stoppage __________
③ to recommend a particular action or plan publicly __________
④ the official residence and office of an ambassador __________
⑤ a promise to do something __________
⑥ a person attempting to be hired, elected, etc. for a position __________
⑦ to outdo someone or something __________
⑧ exceptional, marvelous __________
⑨ a hard substance such as iron and steel __________
⑩ undamaged, uninjured __________

B 단어의 관계에 맞게 빈칸을 채우세요.

① period : periodic = 기간 : __________
② elect : __________ = 선출하다 : 선거
③ __________ : relative = 상대성 : 상대적인
④ polish : polished = 광을 내다 : __________
⑤ entirely : __________ = 전적으로 : 전적인
⑥ patriotic : __________ = 애국적인 : 애국자
⑦ physicist : physics = 물리학자 : __________
⑧ presidential : __________ = 대통령의 : 대통령

C 의미가 같도록 알맞은 단어를 넣어 문장을 완성하세요.

1. He tried to emphasize __________ .
그는 비폭력을 강조하려고 했어.

2. At that time he was __________ a halt to the war.
그 당시에 그는 전쟁 중지를 주장하고 있었어.

3. He has been __________ to a science magazine.
그는 과학 잡지를 정기구독하고 있어.

4. He even read the __________ of Albert Einstein.
그는 심지어 알버트 아인슈타인의 전기도 읽었어.

5. He thinks it is important to know the __________ principles of physics.
그는 물리학의 근본 원리를 아는 것이 중요하다고 생각해.

6. Today he showed me a strange __________ .
오늘 그는 내게 이상한 공식을 보여주었어.

7. He is also making a __________ effort to improve his water rocket.
그는 또 물로켓의 성능을 나아지게 하려고 부단한 노력을 하고 있어.

8. Then he puts it on the shelf to keep it __________ .
그리고는 그는 로켓이 손상되지 않도록 선반에 올려놓아.

D 녹음된 내용을 듣고, 다음 빈칸에 들어갈 단어나 표현을 쓰세요.

Dear Sara,

What ___________ Hoony to change like that? ● He has been ___________ to a science magazine. ● He even read the ___________ of Albert Einstein. ● He thinks it is important to know the ___________ principles of physics. ● Today he showed me a strange __________. ● It was Einstein's theory of ___________. ● Hoony wants to be the first Korean ___________ to win the Nobel Prize. ● He's becoming very ________. ● He is also making a ___________ effort to improve his water rocket. ● He spends __________ too much time experimenting with his rocket. ● Then he puts it on the shelf to keep it ___________. ● He ___________ it with wax every morning.

B o m i : Why are you pasting the ___________ pieces on its body?

Hoony: I'm trying to make my rocket fly for the longest __________ of time. ● I will make this ___________. ● Finally, it will __________ Minsu's.

Sara, does your brother still enjoy making ___________ speeches? ● I hope he gets ___________ school president, competing with 5 other __________. ● Once he makes his ___________ to do well in front of the students, they will vote for him. ● He will ________ his goal of being elected. ● I remember him being quite an __________ speaker. ● He demonstrated his abilities in front of the American __________. ● At that time he was ___________ a ________ to the war. ● He tried to emphasize ___________. ● I'm sure your brother will be a good __________.

Chapter 1 — People

▶ 1단계 : 먼저 그림을 보고, 이 장의 에피소드를 추측해 보세요.

→ **make a commitment to help society** ○

○ **make a historic voyage** ←

→ **long for eternal life** ○

○ **be one's subordinate** ←

Episode

Bomi: Sara, who do you think are some of the world's most influential people? ● And what qualities distinguish them? ● How did Bill Gates earn such an astronomical amount of money? ● Does he have some kind of intuition that allows him to see the future in business? ● Or is he just a money-oriented person?

Sara: I don't think he is money-oriented. ● He is a philanthropist. ● His foundation benefits many people.

Bomi: Really? So he does have some mercy. ● What's the primary goal of his foundation? ● Does it support prodigies?

Sara: Exactly. It supports future scientists throughout the world.

Bomi: It nurtures future Bill Gates.

Sara: Right. He's made a commitment to help society.

Bomi: Are there any historical figures you are interested in?

Sara: I'd like to meet an adventurer like Columbus. ● I'd like to ask why he ventured out into the unknown world. ● I wonder how he could have made such a historic voyage.

Bomi: I'd like to ask if spices such as pepper were so priceless. ● And I'd like to ask him, "If I brought you a crate of pepper, would you be my subordinate?"

Sara: Interesting. If you met the Chinese Emperor, Shin Huang-di, what would you say?

Bomi: The emperor who longed for eternal life? ● I'd say, "Hey, why don't you stop drinking toxic liquids?" or "Why don't you stop disciplining your army so cruelly?"

Sara: If you said that, you'd be exiled.

Bomi: He should know that he is a tyrant. ● His people were suffering under his regime.

Sara: Right. If he hadn't died early, he could have fled his own country.

Bomi: Exactly. He could have been assassinated.

▶ 3단계 : 외우면서 단어를 2번씩 써보세요!

1 influential [ìnfluénʃəl]
a. 영향력 있는
▶ having a strong influence over somebody or something
▶ influence v. 영향을 미치다 n. 영향(력)

2 quality [kwáləti]
n. 자질
▶ good characteristic, feature

3 astronomical [æ̀strənámikəl]
a. 천문학적인, 천문학의
▶ extremely huge, of cosmic proportions
▶ astronomy n. 천문학

4 intuition [ìntjuíʃən]
n. 직관, 직감
▶ immediate understanding, ability to think ahead
▶ intuitive a. 직관의, 직관력 있는

5 money-oriented [mʌ́ni ɔ́ːrientid]
a. 금전만능의
▶ mainly concerned with money

6 philanthropist [filǽnθrəpist]
n. 박애주의자
▶ a person who tries to help people in trouble and improve the world
▶ philanthropy n. 박애주의, 자선

7 foundation [faundéiʃən]
n. 재단
▶ an organization supported by a large amount of money

▶ 외우면서 단어를 2번씩 써보세요!

8 **mercy** [mə́ːrsi]
n. 자비심
- ▶ pity, compassion shown to others
- ▶ merciful a. 자비로운
- ▶ merciless a. 무자비한

9 **primary** [práimèri]
a. 일차적인, 가장 중요한
- ▶ most important, most essential
- ▶ primarily ad. 첫째로, 우선

10 **prodigy** [prádədʒi]
n. 천재, 신동
- ▶ a person who is extremely gifted at doing something
- ▶ prodigious a. 비범한, 놀라운

11 **throughout** [θruːáut]
prep. ~도처에
- ▶ all through, in every part

12 **nurture** [nə́ːrtʃər]
v. 키우다, 돌보다
- ▶ to take care of, to nourish

13 **commitment** [kəmítmənt]
n. 공약, 헌신
- ▶ a promise to do something, dedication
- ▶ make a commitment 공약하다, 헌신하다

14 **figure** [fígjər]
n. 인물
- ▶ a person, especially a well-known one

▶ **3단계 : 외우면서 단어를 2번씩 써보세요!**

15 adventurer [ædvéntʃərər]
n. 모험가
▶ a person who goes on adventures and explorations
▶ adventure n. 모험
▶ adventurous a. 모험을 좋아하는, 대담한

16 venture [véntʃər]
v. 탐험하다 n. 모험
▶ to travel, to explore

17 voyage [vɔ́iidʒ]
n. 항해 v. 항해하다
▶ a long trip over the sea
▶ voyager n. 항해가

18 priceless [práislis]
a. 매우 귀한
▶ extremely valuable

19 subordinate [səbɔ́ːrdənit]
n. 부하
a. 부하의, 종속의
▶ a person who must obey another

20 emperor [émpərər]
n. 황제
▶ a ruler of an empire
▶ empire n. 제국

21 eternal [itə́ːrnəl]
a. 영원한
▶ forever, never-ending
▶ eternity n. 영원함

22 toxic [tάksik]
a. 유독한, 독(성)의
- ▶ poisonous, very harmful
- ▷ toxin n. 독소

23 discipline [dísəplin]
v. 훈련시키다, 단련시키다
n. 훈련, 기강, 징계
- ▶ to drill, to train to act in accordance with rules
- ▷ disciplinary a. 훈련상의, 훈육의
- ▷ disciplined a. 훈련받은

24 exile [égzail]
v. 추방하다 n. 추방, 망명자
- ▶ to cast someone out from a place

25 tyrant [tάiərənt]
n. 폭군
- ▶ a cruel ruler who rules with fear and strength
- ▷ tyranny n. 폭정
- ▷ tyrannical a. 압제적인, 폭정의

26 regime [reiʒíːm]
n. 정권, 통치기간
- ▶ a form of government, a specific government group

27 flee [fliː]
v. 도피하다
- ▶ to run away, to escape

28 assassinate [əsǽsənèit]
v. 암살하다
- ▶ to kill an important person on purpose
- ▷ assassination n. 암살
- ▷ assassinator n. 암살자

Exercise

A 주어진 뜻에 해당하는 단어를 보기에서 찾아 쓰세요.

> priceless   venture   money-oriented   throughout   nurture
> quality   foundation   subordinate   figure   commitment

① good characteristic, feature   _______________
② mainly concerned with money   _______________
③ an organization supported by a large amount of money   _______________
④ all through, in every part   _______________
⑤ to take care of, to nourish   _______________
⑥ a promise to do something, dedication   _______________
⑦ a person, especially a well-known one   _______________
⑧ to travel, to explore   _______________
⑨ to extremely valuable   _______________
⑩ a person who must obey another   _______________

B 단어의 관계에 맞게 빈칸을 채우세요.

① tyrant : _______________ = 폭군 : 폭정
② toxic : toxin = 독의 : _______________
③ _______________ : eternity = 영원한 : 영원함
④ emperor : empire = _______________ : 제국
⑤ voyage : voyager = 항해 : _______________
⑥ mercy : _______________ = 자비심 : 자비로운
⑦ primary : primarily = _______________ : 첫째로
⑧ _______________ : prodigious = 천재 : 비범한

C 의미가 같도록 알맞은 단어를 넣어 문장을 완성하세요.

1. Exactly. He could have been _______________ .
   맞아. 그는 암살당할 수도 있었을 거야.

2. Right. If he hadn't died early, he could have _______________ his own country.
   맞아. 그가 일찍 죽지 않았다면, 자기 나라에서 도망쳐야 했을 수도 있어.

3. His people were suffering under his _______________ .
   백성들이 그의 정권 하에 고통 받고 있었잖아.

4. If you said that, you'd be _______________ .
   그렇게 말하면, 너는 추방당할 거야.

5. Why don't you stop _______________ your army so cruelly?
   그렇게 잔인하게 군대를 훈련시키는 것 좀 그만두는 게 어때?

6. And I'd like to ask him, "If I brought you a crate of pepper, would you be my _______________ ?"
   "제가 후추 한 상자 가져오면, 제 부하가 되어주겠어요?"라고 물어보고 싶어.

7. I'd like to ask if spices such as pepper were so _______________ .
   나는 후추 같은 향신료가 그렇게 귀했는지 묻고 싶어.

8. Sara, who do you think are some of the world's most _______________ people?
   사라, 세상에서 가장 영향력 있는 사람들은 누구라고 생각해?

D 녹음된 내용을 듣고, 다음 빈칸에 들어갈 단어나 표현을 쓰세요.

Bomi: Sara, who do you think are some of the world's most ___________ people? ● And what ___________ distinguish them? ● How did Bill Gates earn such an ___________ amount of money? ● Does he have some kind of ___________ that allows him to see the future in business? ● Or is he just a ___________ person?

Sara: I don't think he is money-oriented. ● He is a ___________. ● His ___________ benefits many people.

Bomi: Really? So he does have some ___________. ● What's the ___________ goal of his foundation? ● Does it support ___________?

Sara: Exactly. It supports future scientists ___________ the world.

Bomi: It ___________ future Bill Gates.

Sara: Right. He's made a ___________ to help society.

Bomi: Are there any historical ___________ you are interested in?

Sara: I'd like to meet an ___________ like Columbus. ● I'd like to ask why he ___________ out into the unknown world. ● I wonder how he could have made such a historic ___________.

Bomi: I'd like to ask if spices such as pepper were so ___________. ● And I'd like to ask him, "If I brought you a crate of pepper, would you be my ___________?"

Sara: Interesting. If you met the Chinese ___________, Shin Huang-di, what would you say?

Bomi: The emperor who longed for ___________ life? ● I'd say, "Hey, why don't you stop drinking ___________ liquids?" or "Why don't you stop ___________ your army so cruelly?"

Sara: If you said that, you'd be ___________.

Bomi: He should know that he is a ___________. ● His people were suffering under his ___________.

Sara: Right. If he hadn't died early, he could have ___________ his own country.

Bomi: Exactly. He could have been ___________. ●

Chapter

1 People

▶ 1단계 : 먼저 그림을 보고, 이 장의 에피소드를 추측해 보세요.

→ **be late for an appointment**

have to pay overdue charges ←

→ **be upset by reckless driver**

▶ 2단계 : 녹음 내용을 들으며, 추측한 에피소드와 비교해 보세요. 

Dear Diary,

Is it possible to find our ideal spouse? ● My mom and dad are not similar at all; in fact, their behaviors contrast in many ways. ● My dad is very punctual. ● He is almost never late for his appointments. ● But mom is always tardy when she goes to meet him. ● Dad thinks it's because she lingers over coffee with her acquaintances. ● If I were my dad, I would be late purposely in revenge. ● Usually my dad is more prudent than my mom, except while driving. ● It's dad who carefully checks all our outgoings. ● It's mom who often has to pay overdue charges for her cell phone. ● She complains that due dates should be extended. ● Consequently, they have arguments over these matters.

This morning my dad declared he is going to apply for auto banking services for her. ● Mom remarked that ideal couples should have a close bond. ● I wonder why so many couples have more contrasts than similarities. ● My grandparents say that a husband and wife should complement each other. ● In some respects, I agree with them. ● My dad is a bit temperamental. ● While driving, he is easily upset by reckless drivers. ● Then he accelerates, trying to frighten them. ● He even wants verbal confirmation that they are wrong. ● It's mom who always persuades dad to calm down. ● She has a talent for soothing him.

▶ 3단계 : 외우면서 단어를 2번씩 써보세요!

1 spouse [spáus]

n. 배우자

▶ a person one is married to, partner, husband or wife

2 contrast [kántræst]

v. 대조되다 n. 대조

▶ to be very different
▶ contrastive a. 대조적인

3 punctual [pʌ́ŋktʃuəl]

a. 시간을 잘 지키는

▶ being prompt and on time
▶ punctuality n. 시간 엄수

4 appointment [əpɔ́intmənt]

n. 약속

▶ a meeting with one or more people

5 tardy [tɑ́ːrdi]

a. 늦은, 지각하는

▶ late, doing something later than one should
▶ tardiness n. 지각 ▶ tardily ad. 늦게

6 linger [líŋgər]

v. 꾸물거리다

▶ to take a longer time to do something than one should
▶ lingering a. 우물쭈물하는

7 acquaintance [əkwéintəns]

n. 아는 사람

▶ a person that you have met and know slightly, but not well
▶ acquaint v. 알게 하다
▶ acquainted a. 안면이 있는, ~에 정통한

8 revenge [rivéndʒ]

n. 복수

▶ punishment done to a person who has done something bad to you
▶ revengeful a. 복수심에 불타는
▶ in revenge 복수로

9 prudent [prúːdənt]

a. 신중한

▶ sensible and careful
▶ prudence n. 신중함

10 outgoings [áutgòuiŋz]

n. 지출

▶ all the money that a person or family spends

11 overdue [òuvərdjúː]

a. 지불 기한이 넘은

▶ late, not paid for on time

12 complain [kəmpléin]

v. 불평하다

▶ to express one's dissatisfaction, to grumble
▶ complaint n. 불평

13 extend [iksténd]

v. 연장하다

▶ to give extra time
▶ extension n. 연장

14 consequently [kɑ́nsikwəntli]

ad. 결과적으로, 따라서

▶ as a result of something
▶ consequence n. 결과
▶ consequent a. 결과의

15 auto banking
[ɔ́ːtou bǽŋkiŋ]
자동 이체
▶ the system that has the bank pay one's bills on the same day each month

_______________ _______________

16 bond [bɑnd]
n. 유대, 유대감
▶ a feeling of friendship and love between people

_______________ _______________

17 similarity [sìməlǽrəti]
n. 유사점, 비슷한 점
▶ alikeness, closeness
▷ similar a. 유사한, 비슷한

_______________ _______________

18 complement [kámpləmənt]
v. 보완하다
▶ to make a good combination
▷ complementary a. 보완하는, 보완적인

_______________ _______________

19 respect [rispékt]
n. 측면
▶ an aspect, a way
▷ in some respects 어떤 면에서

_______________ _______________

20 temperamental [tèmpərəméntl]
a. 변덕스러운, 기질상의
▶ moody, changing quickly from happiness to anger
▷ temperament n. 성격, 기질

_______________ _______________

21 reckless [réklis]
a. 무모한
▶ careless and dangerous, not careful
▷ recklessly ad. 무모하게

_______________ _______________

▶ 외우면서 단어를 2번씩 써보세요!

22 accelerate [æksélərèit]

v. 가속하다

▶ to go faster
▶ acceleration n. 가속
▶ accelerator n. 가속장치

_____________________ _____________________

23 frighten [fráitn]

v. 놀라게 하다, 두려워지게 하다

▶ to scare someone
▶ fright n. 공포
▶ frightened a. 놀란

_____________________ _____________________

24 verbal [və́:rbəl]

a. 말의, 구두의

▶ spoken, oral
▶ verbally ad. 말로, 구두로

_____________________ _____________________

25 confirmation [kànfərméiʃən]

n. 확인, 승인

▶ verification, approval of something
▶ confirm v. 확인하다

_____________________ _____________________

26 persuade [pə:rswéid]

v. 설득하다

▶ to give someone a good reason to
  do something
▶ persuasion n. 설득
▶ persuasive a. 설득력 있는

_____________________ _____________________

27 soothe [su:ð]

v. 진정시키다

▶ to make an angry or upset person
  feel better
▶ soothing a. 진정시키는, 달래는

_____________________ _____________________

Exercise

A 주어진 뜻에 해당하는 단어를 보기에서 찾아 쓰세요.

> overdue complement reckless spouse outgoings
> respect accelerate temperamental bond appointment

① a person one is married to, partner, husband or wife ________________
② a meeting with one or more people ________________
③ all the money that a person or family spends ________________
④ late, not paid for on time ________________
⑤ a feeling of friendship and love between people ________________
⑥ to make a good combination ________________
⑦ an aspect, a way ________________
⑧ moody, changing quickly from happiness to anger ________________
⑨ careless and dangerous, not careful ________________
⑩ to go faster ________________

B 단어의 관계에 맞게 빈칸을 채우세요.

① soothe : ________________ = 진정시키다 : 진정시키는
② verbal : verbally = 말의 : ________________
③ frighten : fright = 놀라게 하다 : ________________
④ ________________ : contrastive = 대조 : 대조적인
⑤ tardy : ________________ = 늦은 : 늦게
⑥ linger : lingering = 꾸물거리다 : ________________
⑦ ________________ : prudence = 신중한 : 신중함
⑧ ________________ : complaint = 불평하다 : 불평

C 의미가 같도록 알맞은 단어를 넣어 문장을 완성하세요.

1. It's mom who always ________________ dad to calm down.
   엄마는 항상 아빠가 침착하시도록 설득하셔.

2. He even wants verbal ________________ that they are wrong.
   그는 심지어 그들이 틀렸다고 말로 확인해주고 싶어서.

3. In some ________________ , I agree with them.
   어떤 면에서, 나는 그분들의 의견에 동의해.

4. This morning my dad declared he is going to apply for ________ services for her.
   오늘 아침에 그는 그녀를 위해서 자동 이체 서비스를 신청할 거라고 말씀하셨어.

5. ________________ , they have arguments over these matters.
   그래서, 그들은 이런 문제에 대해서 말다툼하셔.

6. It's mom who often has to pay ________________ charges for her cell phone.
   종종 휴대 전화 연체 요금을 내야 하는 사람은 엄마야.

7. Usually my dad is more ________________ than my mom, except while driving.
   보통 우리 아빠는 운전할 때를 제외하고는 엄마보다 더 조심스러워.

8. My dad is very ________________ .
   우리 아빠는 상당히 시간을 잘 지키셔.

D 녹음된 내용을 듣고, 다음 빈칸에 들어갈 단어나 표현을 쓰세요.

Dear Diary,

Is it possible to find our ideal __________? ● My mom and dad are not similar at all; in fact, their behaviors _____________ in many ways. ● My dad is very ________. ● He is almost never late for his _____________. ● But mom is always ________ when she goes to meet him. ● Dad thinks it's because she ________ over coffee with her _____________. ● If I were my dad, I would be late purposely in ________. ● Usually my dad is more ___________ than my mom, except while driving. ● It's dad who carefully checks all our ___________. ● It's mom who often has to pay _________ charges for her cell phone. ● She ___________ that due dates should be _________. ● _____________, they have arguments over these matters.

This morning my dad declared he is going to apply for __________ __________ services for her. ● Mom remarked that ideal couples should have a close _______________. ● I wonder why so many couples have more contrasts than _________________. ● My grandparents say that a husband and wife should _______________ each other. ● In some ___________, I agree with them. ● My dad is a bit _____________. ● While driving, he is easily upset by _____________ drivers. ● Then he accelerates, trying to _____________ them. ● He even wants ________ _________ that they are wrong. ● It's mom who always ____________ dad to calm down. ● She has a talent for _______________ him.

Total
/ 30

■ 녹음을 듣고, 해당하는 단어와 뜻을 쓰세요.

1	단어:	뜻:	2	단어:	뜻:
3	단어:	뜻:	4	단어:	뜻:
5	단어:	뜻:	6	단어:	뜻:
7	단어:	뜻:	8	단어:	뜻:
9	단어:	뜻:	10	단어:	뜻:
11	단어:	뜻:	12	단어:	뜻:
13	단어:	뜻:	14	단어:	뜻:
15	단어:	뜻:	16	단어:	뜻:
17	단어:	뜻:	18	단어:	뜻:
19	단어:	뜻:	20	단어:	뜻:
21	단어:	뜻:	22	단어:	뜻:
23	단어:	뜻:	24	단어:	뜻:
25	단어:	뜻:	26	단어:	뜻:
27	단어:	뜻:	28	단어:	뜻:
29	단어:	뜻:	30	단어:	뜻:

접두사 extra- / de-

extra-는 'outside'라는 뜻의 접두사로, '어떤 범위 이외 혹은 이상'이라는 뜻의 단어를 만든다.
de-는 'un-'과 같은 뜻으로, 단어 앞에 붙어 '반대'의 의미를 나타낸다.

extra-

curricular 교과과정의
extra + curricular = extracurricular 과외활동의
ex) Fencing is now a part of the school's extracurricular activities.
이제는 펜싱이 학교 과외활동에 포함된다.

literary 문학의	extraliterary 문학밖의
ordinary 평범한	extraordinary 비상한
marital 결혼의, 부부의	extramarital 혼외의, 불륜의
judicial 재판의	extrajudicial 사법 관할 밖의
terrestrial 지구의	extraterrestrial 지구 밖의
cellular 세포의	extracellular 세포 밖의
legal 법적인	extralegal 법률의 지배를 받지 않는

de-

code 암호화하다
de + code = decode 암호문을 풀다
ex) The teacher couldn't decode the student's note.
선생님은 암호화된 학생의 쪽지를 풀 수 없었다.

compose 조립하다	decompose 분해시키다
certify 인증하다	decertify 인가를 취소하다
caffeinated 카페인을 함유한	decaffeinated 카페인을 제거한
frost 얼리다	defrost 녹이다
centralize 집중시키다	decentralize 분산시키다
hydrated 함수의	dehydrated 탈수한
forestation 조림	deforestation 삼림 벌채

Culture Plus

At a Music Concert 음악회에서

+ **opera singer** 성악가

+ **symphony orchestra** 교향악단

+ **conductor / maestro** 지휘자

+ **company / troupe** 공연단

+ **intermission** 휴식 시간

+ **give a standing ovation** 기립 박수를 치다

+ **call for an encore** 앙코르를 청하다

Chapter 2

History, Art, and Culture

History, Art, and Culture

▶ 1단계 : 먼저 그림을 보고, 이 장의 에피소드를 추측해 보세요.

→ **portray a contemplative person**

figure out the underlying meaning ←

→ **give someone concrete concepts**

Episode

Dear Sara,

Sara, how do you appreciate pieces of art? ● My class went to a gallery. ● I saw a sculpture, *The thinker*, by Rodin. ● What did Rodin try to portray? ● What made this work, *The thinker*, his masterpiece? ● Did he want to portray a contemplative person? ● *The thinker* looked uncomfortable. ● I guess *The thinker* symbolizes a vulnerable person. ● I can't judge whether the sculpture has perfect proportions or not. ● Once I molded a tiny artwork with mud. ● It was not symmetrical at all. ● There were many cracks in it. ● The mud didn't have enough moisture. ● I had to spend a few days completing the ugly piece. ● Rodin must have worked vigorously to finish his great artwork.

Later I stood in front of some abstract paintings. ● Hmmm, how can I evaluate them? ● I tried to figure out their underlying meaning, but they were really ambiguous. ● Some paintings were really hard to comprehend. ● Our teacher said they depicted our subconscious. ● How can I grasp invisible things? ● "These paintings are vague," I said to myself.

Finally, I moved to where there were paintings with vivid colors. ● They were comparatively easy to understand. ● They gave me concrete concepts. ● They were different from the preceding artworks. ● Now I was able to have a mutual understanding with the painters.

▶ 3단계 : 외우면서 단어를 2번씩 써보세요!

1 appreciate [əprí:ʃièit]
v. 감상하다, 평가하다, 감사하다
▶ to recognize good qualities or worth
▶ appreciation n. 감상, 평가, 감사

2 gallery [gǽləri]
n. 미술관, 화랑
▶ a building where artworks are displayed

3 sculpture [skʌ́lptʃər]
n. 조각품
▶ an artwork made from solid materials (not paint)
▶ sculpt v. 조각하다
▶ sculptor n. 조각가

4 portray [pɔːrtréi]
v. 표현하다, 그리다
▶ to explain something using art instead of words
▶ portrayal n. 그리기, 묘사
▶ portrait n. 초상화

5 masterpiece [mǽstərpìːs]
n. 걸작
▶ the best piece of work made by an artist

6 contemplative [kəntémplətiv]
a. 사색하는
▶ thinking very hard and deeply
▶ contemplate v. 묵상하다, 사색하다
▶ contemplation n. 묵상, 사색

7 uncomfortable [ʌ̀nkʌ́mfərtəbəl]
a. 불편한, 마음이 편치 못한
▶ not relaxed, opposite of comfortable

8 vulnerable [vʌ́lnərəbəl]

a. 상처입기 쉬운, 연약한

▶ can be easily harmed, weak and unprotected
▶ vulnerability n. 취약성, 상처 받기 쉬움

_______________ _______________

9 proportion [prəpɔ́ːrʃən]

n. 비율

▶ the balance between parts of the whole
▶ proportional a. 비례하는, 비례의
▶ proportionate a. 비례하는, 균형 잡힌

_______________ _______________

10 mold [mould]

v. 형태를 만들다, 주조하다

▶ to use a material and shape it with one's hands

_______________ _______________

11 symmetrical [simétrikəl]

a. 대칭의

▶ matching perfectly on both sides
▶ symmetry n. 대칭

_______________ _______________

12 crack [kræk]

n. 균열 v. 금이 가다

▶ a thin gap or split in an object, damage

_______________ _______________

13 moisture [mɔ́istʃər]

n. 수분

▶ dampness, wateriness
▶ moist a. 습한, 습기 있는

_______________ _______________

14 complete [kəmplíːt]

v. 완성하다, 완수하다

▶ to finish
▶ completion n. 완성, 완료

_______________ _______________

15 vigorously [vígərəsli]

ad. 원기 왕성하게

▶ energetically, powerfully
▷ vigor n. 원기
▷ vigorous a. 원기 왕성한

16 abstract [æbstrǽkt]

a. 추상적인

▶ conceptual, not concrete
▷ abstraction n. 추상, 추상주의 작품

17 evaluate [ivǽljuèit]

v. 평가하다

▶ to decide if something is good or bad
▷ evaluation n. 평가

18 underlying [ʌ̀ndərláiiŋ]

a. 저변에 깔린, 기초(근본)적인

▶ basic, fundamental and concealed
▷ underlie v. 기초가 되다

19 ambiguous [æmbígjuəs]

a. 애매한, 중의적인

▶ confusing and not clear, vague
▷ ambiguity n. 애매함

20 comprehend [kàmprihénd]

v. 이해하다

▶ to understand
▷ comprehension n. 이해
▷ comprehensive a. 이해력이 있는, 포괄적인

21 subconscious [sʌbkánʃəs]

n. 잠재의식 a. 잠재의식의

▶ inner thoughts that one has but they are not aware of
▷ subconsciousness n. 잠재의식
▷ subconsciously ad. 잠재의식으로

▶ 외우면서 단어를 2번씩 써보세요!

22 invisible [invízəbəl]

a. 보이지 않는

▶ unable to be seen
▷ invisibility n. 눈에 보이지 않음

23 vague [veig]

a. 모호한, 애매한

▶ difficult to understand because the meaning is not explained well

24 vivid [vívi]

a. 생생한

▶ bright and colorful
▷ vividness n. 생생함

25 comparatively [kəmpǽrətivli]

ad. 비교적

▶ relatively, rather
▷ compare v. 비교하다
▷ comparison n. 비교

26 concrete [kánkríːt]

a. 구체적인

▶ real, definite, specific, opposite of abstract

27 preceding [priːsíːdiŋ]

a. 이전의

▶ earlier, former
▷ precede v. 앞서다, 먼저 일어나다
▷ precedent n. 선례

28 mutual [mjúːtʃuəl]

a. 상호의

▶ shared by both of two people
▷ mutuality n. 상호관계, 상관

Exercise

A 주어진 뜻에 해당하는 단어를 보기에서 찾아 쓰세요.

> gallery   portray   vulnerable   proportion   mold
> crack   evaluate   subconscious   vague   concrete

① can be easily harmed, weak and unprotected   _______________
② a thin gap or split in an object, damage   _______________
③ to use a material and shape it with one's hands   _______________
④ a building where artworks are displayed   _______________
⑤ real, definite, specific, opposite of abstract   _______________
⑥ inner thoughts that one has but they are not aware of   _______________
⑦ difficult to understand because the meaning is not explained well   _______________
⑧ to decide if something is good or bad   _______________
⑨ the balance between parts of the whole   _______________
⑩ to explain something using art instead of words   _______________

B 단어의 관계에 맞게 빈칸을 채우세요.

① appreciate : _______________ = 감상하다 : 감상
② sculpture: sculpt = _______________ : 조각하다
③ contemplative : contemplation = 사색하는 : _______________
④ _______________ : symmetry = 대칭의 : 대칭
⑤ complete : _______________ = 완수하다 : 완성
⑥ invisible : invisibility = _______________ : 보이지 않음
⑦ _______________ : comprehensive = 이해하다 : 포괄적인
⑧ preceding : precede = 이전의 : _______________

C 의미가 같도록 알맞은 단어를 넣어 문장을 완성하세요.

1. What made this work, *The Thinker*, his _______________ ?
   무엇이 이 작품, '생각하는 사람'을 그의 걸작으로 만들었을까?

2. *The thinker* looked _______________ .
   '생각하는 사람'은 불편한 듯 보였어.

3. The mud didn't have enough _______________ .
   진흙에 수분이 충분하지 않았어.

4. Rodin must have worked _______________ to finish his great artwork.
   로댕은 자신의 위대한 작품을 끝내기 위해 틀림없이 왕성하게 작업했을 거야.

5. Later I stood in front of some _______________ paintings.
   나중에 나는 몇몇 추상화 앞에 서게 되었어.

6. I tried to figure out their underlying meaning, but they were really _______________ .
   나는 그것들의 저변에 깔린 의미를 찾아내려고 애를 썼지만, 정말 애매했어.

7. Finally, I moved to where there were paintings with _______________ colors.
   마지막으로, 나는 선명한 색채로 그려진 그림이 있는 곳으로 자리를 옮겼어.

8. Now I was able to have a _______________ understanding with the painters.
   나는 그제서야 화가들과 상호 이해할 수가 있었어.

D 녹음된 내용을 듣고, 다음 빈칸에 들어갈 단어나 표현을 쓰세요.

Dear Sara,

Sara, how do you __________ pieces of art? ● My class went to a ________. ● I saw a __________, *The thinker*, by Rodin. ● What did Rodin try to ________? ● What made this work, *The thinker*, his ____________? ● Did he want to portray a ______________ person? ● *The thinker* looked ______________. ● I guess *The thinker* symbolizes a __________ person. ● I can't judge whether the sculpture has perfect __________ or not. ● Once I _________ a tiny artwork with mud. ● It was not __________ at all. ● There were many ________ in it. ● The mud didn't have enough __________. ● I had to spend a few days __________ the ugly piece. ● Rodin must have worked __________ to finish his great artwork.

Later I stood in front of some __________ paintings. ● Hmmm, how can I _________ them? ● I tried to figure out their ___________ meaning, but they were really ______________. ● Some paintings were really hard to __________. ● Our teacher said they depicted our ________________. ● How can I grasp __________ things? ● "These paintings are ________," I said to myself.

Finally, I moved to where there were paintings with ______ colors. ● They were __________________ easy to understand. ● They gave me __________ concepts. ● They were different from the __________ artworks. ● Now I was able to have a ________ understanding with the painters. ●

Unit 6. There was telepathy between us!

History, Art, and Culture

▶ 1단계 : 먼저 그림을 보고, 이 장의 에피소드를 추측해 보세요.

→ see a herd of cows

be compared to a meek person ←

→ intuit one's thoughts

2단계 : 녹음 내용을 들으며, 추측한 에피소드와 비교해 보세요. 

Dear Diary,

Our family visited a farm full of pastureland. ● The meadow was located in a rural area. ● When we arrived, we saw a herd of cows on the grass. ● And there were many livestock animals.

"I'm going to watch the lambs graze," Hoony said. ● Maybe he was thinking of a fable. ● In the fable, the lamb is always innocent while the wolf is vicious. ● In other stories, the lamb is often naive. ● But sometimes it is compared to a meek person.

Seri and I milked the cows to extract their milk. ● Looking into their eyes, I felt a kind of intimacy. ● I felt as if I were identifying myself with the cows. ● I felt as if there was telepathy between us. ● I felt that I could intuit their thoughts. ● Why do we have to provide humans with milk? ● Why do we have to be harnessed? ● Are we destined to serve them? ● We have been companions of peasants for a long time. ● They should honor us. ● We have been used for plowing. ● We've been exploited for harvesting. ● We've been used for manual labor. ● We've been living in wretched conditions. ● We've consistently given our labor to humans. ● Don't you think we're essential to human's success at farming? ● They seemed to urge me to tell their story. ● What a strange feeling!

▶ 3단계 : 외우면서 단어를 2번씩 써보세요!

1 pastureland [pǽstʃərlənd]
n. 목초지
▶ a grass field where animals can eat the grass

2 meadow [médou]
n. 목초지, 초원
▶ a field where plants and flowers are growing

3 rural [rúərəl]
a. 시골의
▶ countryside, not in the city

4 herd [həːrd]
n. 무리, 떼
▶ a group of animals
▷ a herd of 한 무리의

5 livestock [láivstàk]
n. 가축
▶ farm animals such as cows, pigs and sheep

6 graze [greiz]
v. 풀을 뜯어먹다
▶ to eat grass

7 fable [féibəl]
n. 우화
▶ a story that teaches a moral lesson

8 innocent [ínəsnt]
a. 순수한, 죄없는
▶ angelic, crimeless, not guilty of any wrong
▷ innocence n. 순수, 무죄

▶ 외우면서 단어를 2번씩 써보세요!

⑨ vicious [víʃəs]
a. 사악한
▶ corrupt and cruel, wrong
▷ vice n. 악, 부패

⑩ naive [nɑːíːv]
a. 순진한, 단순한
▶ childlike, frank, innocent, simple

⑪ meek [miːk]
a. 온순한
▶ humble and not proud
▷ meekness n. 온순함

⑫ extract [ikstrǽkt]
v. 뽑다, 짜다 n. 추출물
▶ to take or remove something
▷ extraction n. 뽑아냄, 추출
▷ extractor n. 추출자, 추출 장치

⑬ intimacy [íntəməsi]
n. 친밀감
▶ closeness between people
▷ intimate a. 친밀한

⑭ identify [aidéntəfài]
v. 동일시하다, 구별하다
▶ to think someone or something is closely associated with you
▷ identification n. 동일함, 동화
▷ identity n. 동일함, 신원
▷ identify A with B A를 B와 동일시하다

⑮ telepathy [təlépəθi]
n. 텔레파시
▶ the direct communication of thoughts and feelings between people's minds
▷ telepathic a. 텔레파시의

▶ 3단계 : 외우면서 단어를 2번씩 써보세요!

16 intuit [íntʃu(ː)it]

v. 직관으로 알다

▶ to feel or know something even though nobody tells you
▶ intuition n. 직관력
▶ intuitive a. 직관력 있는, 직관적인

17 provide [prəváid]

v. 제공하다

▶ to give something to someone else
▶ provide A with B A에게 B를 공급하다

18 harness [háːrnis]

v. 마구를 채우다, 이용하다
n. 마구

▶ to put leather ropes around an animal so that one can attach things to it

19 destined [déstind]

a. 예정된, 운명 지어진

▶ planned, predetermined
▶ destiny n. 운명
▶ be destined to+ V ～할 운명이다

20 peasant [pézənt]

n. 농부

▶ a person who works on a farm
▶ peasantry n. 영세농민, 소작인 〈집합적〉

21 honor [ánər]

v. 존중하다

▶ to respect someone
▶ honorable a. 존경할 만한

22 plow [plau]

v. 갈다, 경작하다 n. 쟁기

▶ to dig up ground for cultivation

▶ 외우면서 단어를 2번씩 써보세요!

㉓ exploit [éksplɔit]
v. 이용하다, 착취하다
▶ to take advantage of something for oneself
▶ exploitation n. 이용, 착취

_______________ _______________

㉔ harvest [há:rvist]
v. 추수하다 n. 추수
▶ to take the ripe crop out of the fields

_______________ _______________

㉕ manual [mǽnjuəl]
a. 손으로 하는
n. 소책자, 안내서
▶ done by hand, not automatic
▶ manual labor 육체노동

_______________ _______________

㉖ wretched [rétʃid]
a. 비참한
▶ terrible, very bad

_______________ _______________

㉗ consistently [kənsístəntli]
ad. 일관되게
▶ constantly, invariably
▶ consistency n. 일관성
▶ consistent a. 시종 일관된

_______________ _______________

㉘ essential [isénʃəl]
a. 필수적인
▶ necessary, being needed
▶ essence n. 본질, 진수

_______________ _______________

㉙ urge [ə:rdʒ]
v. 요구하다, 촉구하다
▶ to forcefully ask someone to do something

_______________ _______________

Exercise

A 주어진 뜻에 해당하는 단어를 보기에서 찾아 쓰세요.

> pastureland   meadow   fable   extract   identify
> exploit   urge   naive   harvest   peasant

① to take or remove something　　　　　　　　　　　　________________
② to forcefully ask someone to do something　　　　　________________
③ to think someone or something is closely associated with you　________________
④ childlike, frank, innocent, simple　　　　　　　　　________________
⑤ farm animals such as cows, pigs and sheep　　　　________________
⑥ to take the ripe crop out of the fields　　　　　　　________________
⑦ a story that teaches a moral lesson　　　　　　　　________________
⑧ a person who works on a farm　　　　　　　　　　________________
⑨ a grass field where animals can eat the grass　　　________________
⑩ to take advantage of something for oneself　　　　________________

B 단어의 관계에 맞게 빈칸을 채우세요.

① ________________ : innocence = 순수한 : 순수
② intimacy : ________________ = 친밀감 : 친밀한
③ telepathy : telepathic = 텔레파시 : ________________
④ ________________ : intuition = 직관으로 알다 : 직관력
⑤ destined : destiny = ________________ : 운명
⑥ honor : ________________ = 존중하다 : 존경할 만한
⑦ consistently : consistency = ________________ : 일관성
⑧ vicious : vice = 사악한 : ________________

C 의미가 같도록 알맞은 단어를 넣어 문장을 완성하세요.

1. The meadow was located in a ________________ area.
   그 목초지는 시골에 있었어.

2. When we arrived, we saw a ________________ of cows on the grass.
   우리가 도착했을 때, 한 무리의 소들이 풀밭에 있는 것을 보았어.

3. And there were many ________________ animals.
   그리고 거기에는 가축들도 많았어.

4. But sometimes it is compared to a ________________ person.
   하지만 때로 온순한 사람에 비유되기도 해.

5. Why do we have to ________________ humans with milk?
   왜 우리가 인간에게 우유를 제공해줘야 하지?

6. Why do we have to be ________________ ?
   왜 우리가 이용되어야 하지?

7. We have been used for ________________ .
   우리는 밭을 가는 데 이용되어 왔어.

8. We've been living in ________________ conditions.
   우리는 비참한 조건에서 살아왔어.

D 녹음된 내용을 듣고, 다음 빈칸에 들어갈 단어나 표현을 쓰세요.

Dear Diary,

Our family visited a farm full of _____________. ● The ___________ was located in a __________ area. ● When we arrived, we saw a _________ of cows on the grass. ● And there were many _____________ animals.

"I'm going to watch the lambs ____________," Hoony said. ● Maybe he was thinking of a _________. ● In the fable, the lamb is always ___________ while the wolf is __________. ● In other stories, the lamb is often ________. ● But sometimes it is compared to a _________ person.

Seri and I milked the cows to _________ their milk. ● Looking into their eyes, I felt a kind of _________. ● I felt as if I were ___________ myself with the cows. ● I felt as if there was _________ between us. ● I felt that I could _________ their thoughts. ● Why do we have to ___________ humans with milk? ● Why do we have to be ________? ● Are we _________ to serve them? ● We have been companions of __________ for a long time. ● They should _______ us. ● We have been used for ____________. ● We've been ___________ for ___________. ● We've been used for ________ labor. ● We've been living in ________ conditions. ● We've ________ given our labor to humans. ● Don't you think we're ________ to human's success at farming? ● They seemed to ___________ me to tell their story. ● What a strange feeling!

Chapter 2

History, Art, and Culture

▶ 1단계 : 먼저 그림을 보고, 이 장의 에피소드를 추측해 보세요.

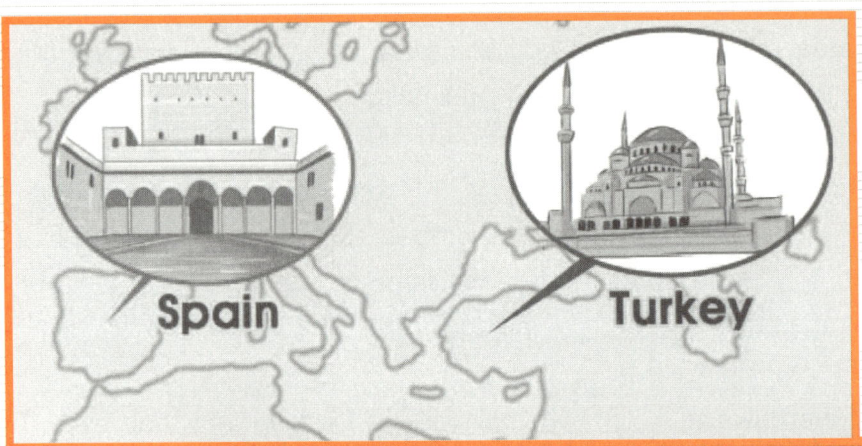

Dear Bomi,

What a splendid culture Turkey has! • Turkey is an integrated place. • It is a great place to experience both Oriental and Western cultures. • It has also been influenced by Islamic culture. • Islamic culture has really flourished in Turkey. • The Turkish people are religious. • During Ramadan, they fast. • They pray five times a day. • There are many mosques, which are sacred places like churches. • The mosques are aesthetically beautiful. • The tiles of the mosques show geometric patterns.

Bomi, what do you think about Islamic culture? • Don't you have any prejudices about it? • Before my trip, I only had superficial knowledge. • I just knew that pork is taboo there. • I just overlooked their culture. • I didn't know that Muslims had established many trading routes. • In terms of trading, they were real pioneers. • I'm sure many people have underestimated their majestic culture.

Isn't it a great pity that information about their cultural legacies are not shown accurately? • Their history seems to have been distorted. • I didn't know that films and TV programs just provide insufficient information. • For example, Muslims were often depicted as terrorists. • Some programs just focused on the terrorists' invasion. • Or they even feature places with unsanitary conditions, not beautiful palaces or their culture. • Do they encourage us to be biased about Islamic culture?

Tomorrow we will go to Spain. • We will visit the famous Islamic architecture, the Alhambra. • It's one of the great tourist attractions. • I won't forget to send you the pictures of it.

▶ **3단계 : 외우면서 단어를 2번씩 써보세요!**

1 splendid [spléndid]
a. 찬란한
▶ very impressive and excellent
▷ splendor n. 훌륭함
▷ splendidly ad. 찬란하게

2 integrated [íntəgrèitid]
a. 통합된
▶ mixed, blended, merged
▷ integrate v. 통합하다
▷ integration n. 통합

3 Western [wéstərn]
a. 서양의
▶ coming from or associated with Western countries

4 Islamic [islǽmik]
a. 이슬람교의
▶ associated with the religion of Islam

5 flourish [flə́:riʃ]
v. 번창하다, 융성하다
▶ to be very successful
▷ flourishing a. 번창하는, 융성한

6 religious [rilídʒəs]
a. 종교적인
▶ connected with religion
▷ religion n. 종교

7 fast [fæst]
v. 금식하다 n. 금식
▶ to stop eating for several days or longer
▷ fasting n. 금식

8 pray [prei]
v. 기도하다
▶ to speak to God
▷ prayer n. 기도

⑨ sacred [séikrid]
a. 성스러운
▶ holy, divine

⑩ aesthetically [esθétikəli]
ad. 미적으로
▶ artistically
▶ aesthetic a. 미의, 미적인
▶ aestheticism n. 탐미주의

⑪ geometric [dʒìːəmétrik]
a. 기하학의, 기하학적인
▶ consisting of regular shaped patterns and lines
▶ geometry n. 기하학
▶ geometrically ad. 기하학적으로

⑫ prejudice [prédʒədis]
n. 편견
▶ an unreasonable dislike or preference
▶ prejudiced a. 편견을 가진

⑬ superficial [sùːpərfíʃəl]
a. 피상적인
▶ without depth, having little understanding of something
▶ superficially ad. 피상적으로

⑭ taboo [təbúː]
n. 금기 a. 금기의
▶ a subject or activity which is not allowed or not permitted

⑮ overlook [òuvərlúk]
v. 간과하다
▶ to neglect, to disregard

▶ **3단계 : 외우면서 단어를 2번씩 써보세요!**

16 establish [istǽbliʃ]

v. 확립하다

▶ to create something and make it last
▶ establishment n. 확립

17 pioneer [pàiəníər]

n. 개척자, 선구자

▶ a person who is first involved in an activity

18 underestimate [ʌndəréstəmèit]

v. 과소평가하다

▶ not to appreciate value of something properly
▶ underestimation n. 과소평가

19 majestic [mədʒéstik]

a. 웅장한

▶ impressive, splendid
▶ majesty n. 웅장함. 장엄함

20 legacy [légəsi]

n. 유산

▶ something that is handed down from someone else, heritage

21 accurately [ǽkjərətli]

ad. 정확하게

▶ correctly, exactly
▶ accuracy n. 정확(성)
▶ accurate a. 정확한

22 distort [distɔ́ːrt]

v. 왜곡하다

▶ to change something to make it look bad
▶ distortion n. 왜곡

▶ 외우면서 단어를 2번씩 써보세요!

23 insufficient [ìnsəfíʃənt]
a. 불충분한

▶ not having enough of something
▶ insufficiency n. 불충분
▶ insufficiently ad. 불충분하게

24 depict [dipíkt]
v. 묘사하다

▶ to describe something
▶ depiction n. 묘사
▶ depictive a. 묘사적인

25 invasion [invéiʒən]
n. 침략

▶ an action of taking an army into another country
▶ invade v. 침략하다

26 unsanitary [ʌ̀nsǽnətèri]
a. 비위생적인

▶ dirty, unclean
▶ sanitary a. 위생적인
▶ sanitation n. 위생

27 biased [báiəst]
a. 편견을 가진

▶ judging something unfairly, prejudiced
▶ bias v. 편견을 갖게 하다 n. 편견, 선입견

28 architecture [á:rkətèktʃər]
n. 건축물

▶ the design and style of a building
▶ architect n. 건축가
▶ architectural a. 건축의

29 attraction [ətrǽkʃən]
n. 관광지, 매력

▶ a famous thing that people come to see
▶ attract v. 주의를 끌다
▶ attractive a. 매력적인

Exercise

A 주어진 뜻에 해당하는 단어를 보기에서 찾아 쓰세요.

> Western   fast   geometric   superficial   taboo
> pioneer   underestimate   legacy   invasion   biased

① consisting of regular shaped patterns and lines ____________________
② not to appreciate value of something properly ____________________
③ a subject or activity which is not allowed or not permitted ____________________
④ judging something unfairly, prejudiced ____________________
⑤ to stop eating for several days or longer ____________________
⑥ something that is handed down from someone else, heritage ____________________
⑦ an action of taking an army into another country ____________________
⑧ a person who is first involved in an activity ____________________
⑨ coming from or associated with Western countries ____________________
⑩ without depth, having little understanding of something ____________________

B 단어의 관계에 맞게 빈칸을 채우세요.

① ____________________ : splendor = 찬란한 : 훌륭함
② integrated : integrate = 통합된 : ____________________
③ pray: prayer = 기도하다 : ____________________
④ aesthetically : ____________________ = 미적으로 : 탐미주의
⑤ establish : establishment = ____________________ : 확립
⑥ accurately : ____________________ = 정확하게 : 정확(성)
⑦ ____________________ : depictive = 묘사하다 : 묘사적인
⑧ unsanitary : sanitary = 비위생적인 : ____________________

C 의미가 같도록 알맞은 단어를 넣어 문장을 완성하세요.

1. Islamic culture has really ____________________ in Turkey.
   이슬람 문화는 터키에서 정말 융성했어.

2. The Turkish people are ____________________ .
   터키 사람들은 종교적이야.

3. There are many mosques, which are ____________________ places like churches.
   모스크가 많은데, 그곳은 교회처럼 성스러운 장소야.

4. Don't you have any ____________________ about it?
   그것에 대해 편견을 가지고 있지는 않니?

5. I'm sure many people have underestimated their ____________________ culture.
   나는 많은 사람들이 그들의 웅장한 문화를 과소평가했다고 확신해.

6. Their history seems to have been ____________________ .
   그들의 역사는 왜곡된 것 같아.

7. I didn't know that films and TV programs just provide ____________ information.
   나는 영화와 TV 프로그램에서 충분한 정보를 주고 있지 않는다는 것을 몰랐어.

8. It's one of the great tourist ____________________ .
   그곳은 아주 유명한 관광지 중 하나야.

D 녹음된 내용을 듣고, 다음 빈칸에 들어갈 단어나 표현을 쓰세요.

Dear Bomi,

What a _________ culture Turkey has! ● Turkey is an __________ place. ●

It is a great place to experience both Oriental and _________ cultures. ● It has also been influenced by _________ culture. ● Islamic culture has really __________ in Turkey. ● The Turkish people are _________. ● During Ramadan, they _____. ● They ______ five times a day. ● There are many mosques, which are _________ places like churches. ● The mosques are ___________ beautiful. ● The tiles of the mosques show __________ patterns.

Bomi, what do you think about Islamic culture? ● Don't you have any __________ about it? ● Before my trip, I only had __________ knowledge. ● I just knew that pork is ______ there. ● I just __________ their culture. ● I didn't know that Muslims had __________ many trading routes. ● In terms of trading, they were real _________. ● I'm sure many people have _______________ their _________ culture.

Isn't it a great pity that information about their cultural __________ are not shown __________? ● Their history seems to have been _________. ● I didn't know that films and TV programs just provide __________ information. ● For example, Muslims were often _________ as terrorists. ● Some programs just focused on the terrorists' _________. ● Or they even feature places with __________ conditions, not beautiful palaces or their culture. ● Do they encourage us to be _______ about Islamic culture?

Tomorrow we will go to Spain. ● We will visit the famous Islamic __________, the Alhambra. ● It's one of the great tourist __________. ● I won't forget to send you the pictures of it.

Chapter 2

Unit 8. Home decorating is not easy.

History, Art, and Culture

→ have a career as a designer

make a room more decorative ←

→ choose a color scheme that typifies someone

2단계 : 녹음 내용을 들으며, 추측한 에피소드와 비교해 보세요. 

Seri: Why don't we change our home decor? ● We can relocate the furniture. ● I can show you how to rearrange your room. ● We can change the wallpaper and make the room more decorative.
Bomi: You look self-confident. ● But I'm not sure I like your design concept.

Seri thinks herself very artistic. ● She believes she is very versatile. ● She likes making crafts. ● She once designed a jewelry box and won a prize. ● She said her jewelry box was designed elaborately. ● She also said it fascinated all the girls. ● She thought her box was sensational. ● I can easily imagine her having a career as a designer. ● For one design contest, she created a bandage with beads attached to it. ● I perceived that it would be totally impractical. ● But she expected that she would get a substantial amount of prize money. ● She said that her bandage would be prominent.

Bomi: Seri, what's your wallpaper color scheme? Would you think of pink?
Seri: What a coincidence! ● How come you came up with the same idea as me? ● This pink fabric will be the best fit for the pink wallpaper, too.
Bomi: But our color scheme can be selective, right? ● I'm very skeptical about your color scheme. ● Why don't you modify your plan?

Then Hoony interjected with his own idea. ● He chose a blue color scheme that typifies him. ● Maybe he was thinking of Superman. ● Hey, Seri and Hoony, maybe we should postpone changing our home decor.

1 decor [deikɔ́ːr]

n. 장식

▶ the style of a house's furnishing and decoration such as wallpaper

2 relocate [riːlóukeit]

v. 위치를 바꾸다

▶ to move something
▶ relocation n. 위치 변경, 재배치

3 rearrange [rìːəréindʒ]

v. 재배치하다, 재배열하다

▶ to change the positions of things
▶ rearrangement n. 재배치

4 wallpaper [wɔ́ːlpèipər]

n. 벽지

▶ the decorative paper on the walls of a room

5 decorative [dékərèitiv]

a. 장식적인

▶ looking pretty and attractive
▶ decorate v. 장식하다
▶ decoration n. 장식

6 self-confident [self kánfidənt]

a. 자신 있는

▶ believing that you can do something well
▶ self-confidence n. 자신감

7 concept [kánsept]

n. 개념

▶ an idea or theme

8 artistic [áːrtístik]

a. 예술적인

▶ good at drawing, painting, or designing things in a beautiful way
▶ artist n. 예술가

▶ 외우면서 단어를 2번씩 써보세요!

9 versatile [və́:rsətl]
a. 다재다능한, 다용도의
▶ having the ability to do many different things well
▶ versatility n. 다재다능, 다용도

10 craft [kræft]
n. 공예품, 수공품
▶ a thing that is made by hand such as pottery or toys
▶ craftwork n. 공예
▶ craftsman n. 장인, 기능공

11 jewelry [dʒúːəlri]
n. 보석류
▶ precious stones and metals
▶ jewel n. 보석
▶ jeweled a. 보석으로 장식한

12 elaborately [ilǽbərèitli]
ad. 정교하게, 공들여서
▶ intricately, elegantly
▶ elaborate a. 공들인, 정교한

13 fascinate [fǽsənèit]
v. 마음을 사로잡다, 황홀하게 하다
▶ to get people's attention
▶ fascination n. 매혹, 매료
▶ fascinating a. 매혹적인

14 sensational [senséiʃənəl]
a. 선풍적인
▶ remarkable, causing great excitement and interest
▶ sensation n. 세상을 떠들썩하게 함
▶ sensationally ad. 선풍적으로

15 career [kəríər]
n. 직업, 경력
▶ a job that one has for a long time

▶ **3단계 : 외우면서 단어를 2번씩 써보세요!**

16 bead [biːd]
n. 구슬
▶ a small piece of colored glass, plastic or stone
▶ beading n. 구슬 세공
▶ beaded a. 구슬 장식한

17 perceive [pərsíːv]
v. 알아차리다, 인지하다
▶ to be aware of something
▶ perception n. 인지
▶ perceptible a. 인지할 수 있는

18 impractical [impræktikəl]
a. 비실용적인
▶ unrealistic, absurd, opposite of practical

19 substantial [səbstǽnʃəl]
a. 상당한
▶ abundant, ample
▶ substantially ad. 상당히

20 prominent [prámənənt]
a. 두드러진, 눈길을 끄는
▶ easily seen, eye-catching
▶ prominence n. 두드러짐, 탁월함

21 color scheme [kʌ́lər skiːm]
색 배합
▶ a combination of several colors that one chooses to decorate something with

22 coincidence [kouínsədəns]
n. 우연의 일치
▶ a situation in which related events happen at the same time
▶ coincidental a. 일치하는, 동시에 일어나는
▶ coincidentally ad. 우연의 일치로

▶ 외우면서 단어를 2번씩 써보세요!

23 come up with [kʌm ʌp wið]
생각해내다
▶ to suggest, to think

24 fabric [fǽbrik]
n. 천, 헝겊
▶ cloth

25 selective [siléktiv]
a. 선택안이 있는, 고르는
▶ choicy, choosy
▷ selectively ad. 선택적으로

26 skeptical [sképtikəl]
a. 회의적인
▶ having doubts about something, unsure of something
▷ skeptic n. 회의론자
▷ skepticism n. 회의론

27 modify [mɑ́dəfài]
v. 수정하다
▶ to change something slightly
▷ modification n. 수정

28 interject [ìntərdʒékt]
v. 끼어들다
▶ to stop someone talking so that you can talk
▷ interjection n. 끼어들기

29 typify [típəfài]
v. 상징하다, 대표하다
▶ to represent something, to characterize
▷ typical a. 전형적인

30 postpone [poustpóun]
v. 연기하다
▶ to put off till later time
▷ postponement n. 연기

Exercise

A 주어진 뜻에 해당하는 단어를 보기에서 찾아 쓰세요.

> decor   wallpaper   craft   sensational   bead
> career   coincidence   interject   modify   impractical

① remarkable, causing great excitement and interest   _______________
② to stop someone talking so that you can talk   _______________
③ a small piece of colored glass, plastic or stone   _______________
④ the decorative paper on the walls of a room   _______________
⑤ unrealistic, absurd, opposite of practical   _______________
⑥ to change something slightly   _______________
⑦ the style of a house's furnishing and decoration such as wallpaper _______________
⑧ a job that one has for a long time   _______________
⑨ a situation in which related events happen at the same time   _______________
⑩ a thing that is made by hand such as pottery or toys   _______________

B 단어의 관계에 맞게 빈칸을 채우세요.

① _________________ : decorate = 장식적인 : 장식하다
② artistic : artist = _________________ : 예술가
③ versatile : versatility = _________________ : 다재다능
④ jewelry : jeweled = 보석 : _________________
⑤ perceive : _________________ = 인지하다 : 인지
⑥ _________________ : prominence = 두드러진 : 탁월함
⑦ skeptical : skeptic = 회의적인 : _________________
⑧ typify : typical = _________________ : 전형적인

C 의미가 같도록 알맞은 단어를 넣어 문장을 완성하세요.

1. We can _________________ the furniture.
   가구 위치를 좀 바꿔볼 수 있잖아.

2. You look _________________ .
   너는 자신 있어 보이는구나.

3. She said her jewelry box was designed _________________ .
   그녀는 자기의 보석함이 정교하게 디자인 되었다고 말했다.

4. But she expected that she would get a ___________ amount of prize money.
   하지만 그녀는 상당한 금액의 상금을 받을 것이라고 기대했다.

5. Seri, what's your wallpaper _________________ ?
   세리, 벽지 색깔은 뭐로 할 거야?

6. How come you _________________ the same idea as me?
   어떻게 나와 같은 생각을 했어?

7. She also said it _________________ all the girls.
   그녀는 또한 그것이 모든 소녀들을 사로잡았다고 했다.

8. Hey, Seri and Hoony, maybe we should _____________ changing our home decor.
   이봐, 세리와 후니, 우리 집안 장식을 바꾸는 것은 좀 뒤로 미루어야겠다.

D 녹음된 내용을 듣고, 다음 빈칸에 들어갈 단어나 표현을 쓰세요.

Seri: Why don't we change our home _______? ● We can ________ the furniture. ● I can show you how to __________ your room. ● We can change the ________ and make the room more _________.

Bomi: You look ______________. ● But I'm not sure I like your design ________.

Seri thinks herself very ________. ● She believes she is very ________. ● She likes making _______. ● She once designed a ________ box and won a prize. ● She said her jewelry box was designed __________. ● She also said it _________ all the girls. ● She thought her box was _________. ● I can easily imagine her having a _______ as a designer. ● For one design contest, she created a bandage with ______ attached to it. ● I _________ that it would be totally _________. ● But she expected that she would get a _________ amount of prize money. ● She said that her bandage would be _________.

Bomi: Seri, what's your wallpaper ______ ________? Would you think of pink?

Seri: What a ______________! ● How come you ________ ______ ______ the same idea as me? ● This pink ________ will be the best fit for the pink wallpaper, too.

Bomi: But our color scheme can be ________, right? ● I'm very _________ about your color scheme. ● Why don't you _______ your plan?

Then Hoony _________ with his own idea. ● He chose a blue color scheme that ________ him. ● Maybe he was thinking of Superman. ● Hey, Seri and Hoony, maybe we should ________ changing our home decor.

Total
/ 30

■ 녹음을 듣고, 해당하는 단어와 뜻을 쓰세요.

1	단어:	뜻:	2	단어:	뜻:
3	단어:	뜻:	4	단어:	뜻:
5	단어:	뜻:	6	단어:	뜻:
7	단어:	뜻:	8	단어:	뜻:
9	단어:	뜻:	10	단어:	뜻:
11	단어:	뜻:	12	단어:	뜻:
13	단어:	뜻:	14	단어:	뜻:
15	단어:	뜻:	16	단어:	뜻:
17	단어:	뜻:	18	단어:	뜻:
19	단어:	뜻:	20	단어:	뜻:
21	단어:	뜻:	22	단어:	뜻:
23	단어:	뜻:	24	단어:	뜻:
25	단어:	뜻:	26	단어:	뜻:
27	단어:	뜻:	28	단어:	뜻:
29	단어:	뜻:	30	단어:	뜻:

접두사 post-와 어근 -pos / -spect

-pos는 'to put'이라는 뜻의 어근으로, '어떤 위치나 상태에 놓다'는 뜻의 단어를 만든다.
post-는 'behind'라는 뜻의 접두사로, '어떤 시점 후에 발생하다'는 뜻의 단어를 만든다.
-spect는 'look'이라는 뜻의 어근으로,'바라보거나 주의를 기울이다'는 뜻의 단어를 만든다.

-pos/post-

de- 반대의(un-)
de + pose = depose 물러나게 하다
ex) Soon, the king was deposed from the throne.
곧 왕은 왕위에서 물러나게 되었다.

- **ex-** ~밖으로   **expose** 드러내다, 노출시키다
- **in-** ~안으로   **impose** 의무를 부과하다, 강요하다
- **trans-** 횡단   **transposition** 위치를 바꾸어 넣기
- **war** 전쟁   **postwar** 전후
- **position** 위치   **postposition** 후치, 뒤에 둠
- **graduate** 졸업생   **postgraduate** 대학원 학생
- **modernism** 모더니즘   **postmodernism** 포스트모더니즘

-spect

retro 뒤
retro + spect = retrospect 회상
ex) In retrospect, I wish I'd been nicer to her.
돌이켜 생각해보면, 그녀에게 더 잘해줄 걸 그랬어요.

- **in-** ~안으로   **inspect** 면밀히 살피다
- **ex-** 외부의   **expect** 기대하다
- **pro-** 앞으로   **prospect** 전망
- **re-** 뒤   **respect** 관심, 고려
- **intro-** 안의   **introspection** 자기 관찰
- **ad-** ~를 항하여   **aspect** 관점, 양상
- **circum-** 주위에   **circumspect** 조심성 있는, 용의주도한

Art Movements   미술사조

+ **Classicism** 고전주의

+ **Romanticism** 낭만주의

+ **Impressionism** 인상주의

+ **Cubism** 입체파

+ **Abstract Art** 추상 미술

+ **Realism** 사실주의

+ **Surrealism** 초현실주의

Politics and Social Issues

Unit 9. Hoony thinks girls have illusions about boys.

Politics and Social Issues

▶ 1단계 : 먼저 그림을 보고, 이 장의 에피소드를 추측해 보세요.

→ **be victims of gender discrimination**

pass specific rites of passage ←

→ **wear very feminine clothing**

Dear Diary,

I inferred from Hoony's behavior that something was wrong.

Bomi: What's wrong, Hoony?

Hoony: Why do girls have illusions about boys? ● I didn't realize that gender discrimination is prevalent among girls. ● Why do they think boys should be better at math problems like fractions? ● They think it should be boys who carry heavy objects like recycling bins. ● Why should boys do that? ● We are victims of gender discrimination. ● Sometimes girls treat us like slaves. ● Girls are irresponsible. ● They just pretend that such work is exhausting for them.

I know why Hoony is so sensitive about this issue. ● He is concealing his feelings. ● Hoony is afraid that his new classmate, Taeji, is more appealing to girls. ● Taeji is good at martial arts. ● Before Taeji came to school, Hoony was the most popular boy. ● He doesn't want to surrender his position. ● He wants to secure his position. ● Now he is attributing the girls' attitude to discrimination. ● Sometimes boys have to pass specific rites of passage to prove their physical power. ● They fight because they think that strength is a virtue that boys have. ● They think weak boys are often despised. ● Hoony thinks Taeji hasmore masculine characteristics than him.

Hoony, girls are inclined to like boys who have tender hearts, not big muscles. ● Girls like warm-hearted boys. ● I think you're the ideal type of man. ● Now, he is getting more agitated. ● I always thought that girls were victims of sexism. ● I thought I should always wear very feminine clothing. ● Now I see that boys and girls are equal victims of gender discrimination. ● Hoony made me realize that boys feel social pressure, too.

1 infer [infə́ːr]
v. 추론하다
▶ to guess something; to decide that something is probably true
▷ inference n. 추론

2 illusion [ilúːʒən]
n. 환상, 착각
▶ a false belief or idea
▷ illusory a. 착각의, 착각을 일으키는

3 prevalent [prévələnt]
a. 널리 퍼진, 보급된
▶ widespread, commonly occurring
▷ prevail v. 우세하다, 만연하다
▷ prevalence n. 우세함, 만연함

4 fraction [frǽkʃən]
n. 분수
▶ a number which is expressed as a proportion of two whole numbers

5 recycling [riːsáikliŋ]
n. 재활용
▶ using something again instead of throwing it away
▷ recycle v. 재활용하다

6 victim [víktim]
n. 피해자, 희생자
▶ someone who has been hurt or killed by another person
▷ victimize v. 희생시키다

7 gender discrimination
[dʒéndər diskrìmənéiʃən]
성차별
▶ giving a disadvantage to someone because of their gender

▶ 외우면서 단어를 2번씩 써보세요!

8 slave [sleiv]

n. 노예

▶ someone who is forced to work without pay
▶ slavery n. 노예제도

9 irresponsible [ìrispánsəbə]

a. 무책임한

▶ untrustworthy, careless
▶ irresponsibility n. 무책임

10 exhausting [igzɔ́:stiŋ]

a. 피로하게 하는

▶ difficult and making one tired

11 issue [íʃuː]

n. 논제, 이슈

▶ a fact or important subject that many people discuss

12 conceal [kənsíːl]

v. 숨기다, 은폐하다

▶ to hide something
▶ concealment n. 은폐

13 appealing [əpíːliŋ]

a. 마음을 끄는, 관심을 끄는

▶ attractive to other people
▶ appeal v. 마음을 끌다 n. 매력

14 martial art [máːrʃəl aːrt]

무술

▶ one of the techniques of self-defense such as kung fu or taekwondo
▶ martial artist n. 무술가

15 popular [pápjələr]

a. 인기 있는

▶ being liked by many people
▶ popularity n. 인기

▶ **3단계 : 외우면서 단어를 2번씩 써보세요!**

16 surrender [səréndər]
v. 내주다, 포기하다
▶ to give up something or lose status

17 secure [sikjúər]
v. 지키다, 확보하다
▶ to keep one's status, to make something safe from attack
▶ security n. 보호, 보장, 안전

18 attribute [ətríbjuːt]
v. ~의 탓으로 돌리다   n. 속성, 특징
▶ to think that a situation is caused by a particular thing
▶ attribution n. 귀착시킴, 귀속
▶ attributable a. ~에 기인하는
▶ attribute A to B A를 B의 탓으로 돌리다

19 rite of passage [rait ɔv pǽsidʒ]
통과의례
▶ a tradition or custom that one must follow to gain something

20 virtue [və́ːrtʃuː]
n. 미덕
▶ a behavior or characteristic that people believe is good
▶ virtuous a. 덕 있는, 고결한

21 despise [dispáiz]
v. 무시하다, 얕보다
▶ to have a low opinion of someone or something

22 masculine [mǽskjəlin]
a. 남자다운, 힘센
▶ manly, opposite of feminine
▶ masculinity n. 남성다움

▶ 외우면서 단어를 2번씩 써보세요!

23 inclined [inkláind]

a. ~의 경향이 있는, ~하고 싶어하는

▶ being likely to do something in one way, disposed
▶ inclination n. 경향, 기질
▶ be inclined to+ V ~하는 경향이 있다

24 warm-hearted [wɔːrm háːrtid]

a. 마음이 따뜻한

▶ kind and generous to other people

25 ideal [aidíːəl]

a. 이상적인 n. 이상

▶ the best, perfect
▶ ideally ad. 이상적으로

26 agitated [ǽdʒətèitid]

a. 흥분된, 동요한

▶ angry and upset
▶ agitation n. 흥분, 동요

27 sexism [séksizəm]

n. 성차별

▶ gender discrimination
▶ sexist n. 성차별주의자

28 feminine [fémənin]

a. 여성스러운

▶ womanish, opposite of masculine
▶ femininity n. 여성다움, 여성임

29 equal [íːkwəl]

a. 같은, 동등한

▶ alike, the same, fair
▶ equality n. 동등함

30 social pressure [sóuʃəl préʃər]

사회적 압력

▶ rules and guidelines that other people want you to follow

Exercise

A 주어진 뜻에 해당하는 단어를 보기에서 찾아 쓰세요.

> infer　fraction　issue　exhausting　recycling
> attribute　virtue　despise　inclined　feminine

① a number which is expressed as a proportion of two whole numbers ＿＿＿＿＿＿
② using something again instead of throwing it away ＿＿＿＿＿＿
③ to guess something; to decide that something is probably true ＿＿＿＿＿＿
④ womanish, opposite of masculine ＿＿＿＿＿＿
⑤ a behavior or characteristic that people believe is good ＿＿＿＿＿＿
⑥ difficult and making one tired ＿＿＿＿＿＿
⑦ to have a low opinion of someone or something ＿＿＿＿＿＿
⑧ to think that a situation is caused by a particular thing ＿＿＿＿＿＿
⑨ being likely to do something in one way, disposed ＿＿＿＿＿＿
⑩ a fact or important subject that many people discuss ＿＿＿＿＿＿

B 단어의 관계에 맞게 빈칸을 채우세요.

① illusion : ＿＿＿＿＿＿ = 환상 : 착각의
② prevalent : prevail = ＿＿＿＿＿＿ : 만연하다
③ slave : slavery = 노예 : 노예제도
④ conceal : ＿＿＿＿＿＿ = 숨기다 : 은폐
⑤ secure : ＿＿＿＿＿＿ = 지키다 : 보호
⑥ masculine : masculinity = 남자다운 : ＿＿＿＿＿＿
⑦ ideal : ideally = 이상적인, 이상 : ＿＿＿＿＿＿
⑧ agitated : ＿＿＿＿＿＿ = 흥분된 : 흥분시키다

C 의미가 같도록 알맞은 단어를 넣어 문장을 완성하세요.

1. We are ＿＿＿＿＿＿ of gender discrimination.
우리는 성차별의 피해자야.

2. Girls are ＿＿＿＿＿＿ .
여자아이들은 무책임해.

3. Taeji is good at ＿＿＿＿＿＿ .
태지는 무술을 잘해.

4. He doesn't want to ＿＿＿＿＿＿ his position.
그는 그 자리를 내주고 싶지 않은 거야.

5. Sometimes boys have to pass specific ＿＿＿＿＿＿ to prove their physical power.
남자아이들은 가끔 자신들의 신체적 힘을 증명하기 위해 특정한 통과의례를 거쳐야 해.

6. Girls like ＿＿＿＿＿＿ boys.
여자아이들은 따뜻한 마음을 가진 남자아이들을 좋아해.

7. I always thought that girls were victims of ＿＿＿＿＿＿ .
나는 늘 여자아이들이 성차별의 피해자라고 생각했었어.

8. Hoony made me realize that boys feel ＿＿＿＿＿＿ , too.
후니 때문에 남자아이들도 사회적 압력을 느낀다는 것을 깨닫게 되었어.

D 녹음된 내용을 듣고, 다음 빈칸에 들어갈 단어나 표현을 쓰세요.

Dear Diary,

I __________ from Hoony's behavior that something was wrong.

Bomi: What's wrong, Hoony?

Hoony: Why do girls have __________ about boys? ● I didn't realize that gender discrimination is __________ among girls. ● Why do they think boys should be better at math problems like __________? ● They think it should be boys who carry heavy objects like __________ bins. ● Why should boys do that? ● We are ______ of __________ ____________. ● Sometimes girls treat us like ______. ● Girls are ____________. ● They just pretend that such work is __________ for them.

I know why Hoony is so sensitive about this __________. ● He is ____________ his feelings. ● Hoony is afraid that his new classmate, Taeji, is more __________ to girls. ● Taeji is good at __________ ______. ● Before Taeji came to school, Hoony was the most __________ boy. ● He doesn't want to __________ his position. ● He wants to ________ his position. ● Now he is __________ the girls' attitude to discrimination. ● Sometimes boys have to pass specific ____________________ to prove their physical power. ● They fight because they think that strength is a __________ that boys have. ● They think weak boys are often __________. ● Hoony thinks Taeji has more ____________ characteristics than him. Hoony, girls are __________ to like boys who have tender hearts, not big muscles. ● Girls like warm-hearted boys. ● I think you're the ______ type of man. ● Now, he is getting more __________. ● I always thought that girls were victims of __________. ● I thought I should always wear very __________ clothing. ● Now I see that boys and girls are __________ victims of gender discrimination. ● Hoony made me realize that boys feel   , too. ●

▶ 1단계 : 먼저 그림을 보고, 이 장의 에피소드를 추측해 보세요.

→ **pretend to be courteous**

be involved in bribery scandal ←

→ **be interested in satirical games**

Dear Sara,

What are politicians like? ● What are the requirements to enter parliament? ● What qualifications do they need? ● People who want to become politicians should be given a rigorous interview. ● During the interview, we should check carefully to see if they are two-faced. ● Many politicians seem to have some traits in common. ● They pretend to be courteous. ● They even promise voters that their actions will be transparent. ● But, once they are elected, their policies change. ● Recently, some politicians were involved in bribery scandals. ● Grandpa said that people shouldn't have voted for those nominees. ● Their corrupt actions are very serious. ● I think they should resign immediately. ● When will the Supreme Court intervene in these cases? ● Are the police going to investigate them thoroughly? In cyberspace, we can mock these people in funny ways. ● My friends like writing satirical jokes about them on their webpages. ● These things sweep through our country like an epidemic. ● They illustrate how people feel about corrupt politicians. ● Sometimes government officials at the highest rank are described as animals. ● They are sentenced to life-long imprisonment. ● They have to crawl around like bugs, making apologies. ● We can make them vanish from our view. ● If you're also interested in satirical games and jokes, please let me know.

Sara, I heard America has a two-party system, the Democrats and Republicans. ● Which party shows more support for the rights of minorities such as the handicapped? ● Are both parties strongly against racism? ● I heard the Democrats are more liberal, while Republicans are more conservative. ● Anyway, I hope both parties work for the people.

▶ 3단계 : 외우면서 단어를 2번씩 써보세요!

1 politician [pəlitíʃən]
n. 정치인
▶ a person who is part of the government of a country
▶ politics n. 정치, 정치학
▶ political a. 정치적인

2 requirement [rikwáiərmənt]
n. 요건
▶ a quality or qualification that people need to have
▶ require v. 필요로 하다

3 qualification [kwàləfəkéiʃən]
n. 자격
▶ a special skill
▶ qualify v. 자격을 주다, 자격을 얻다
▶ qualified a. 자격을 갖춘

4 rigorous [rígərəs]
a. 엄격한
▶ very thorough, severe
▶ rigor n. 엄격, 준엄
▶ rigorously ad. 엄격하게

5 two-faced [tuː feist]
a. 표리부동한, 위선적인
▶ deceitful, cunning

6 trait [treit]
n. 특성
▶ a particular characteristic that someone has
▶ have (traits) in common ~라는 공통점이 있다(공통적인 특성을 가지고 있다)

7 courteous [kə́ːrtiəs]
a. 정중한
▶ well-mannered, polite
▶ courteously ad. 정중하게

▶ 외우면서 단어를 2번씩 써보세요!

8 transparent [trænspέərənt]
a. 투명한, 정직한
▶ understandable, apparent, easily understood or recognized
▶ transparency n. 투명성

9 policy [pάləsi]
n. 정책
▶ a set of plans used as a basis for an organization

10 bribery [bráibəri]
n. 뇌물수수
▶ the act of giving money to people so that they will do what you want
▶ bribe v. 뇌물을 주다 n. 뇌물

11 nominee [nàməní:]
n. 지명자
▶ a person who other people recommend for a job
▶ nominate v. 지명하다
▶ nomination n. 지명

12 corrupt [kərΛpt]
a. 부패한, 타락한
v. 타락시키다
▶ morally wrong, dishonest
▶ corruption n. 타락, 부패
▶ corruptible a. 타락하기 쉬운

13 resign [rizáin]
v. 사임하다, 사직하다
▶ to announce that one is leaving a job or position
▶ resignation n. 사임, 사직

14 Supreme Court
[səprí:m kɔ:rt]
대법원
▶ the highest level court where criminals go to trial

▶ 3단계 : 외우면서 단어를 2번씩 써보세요!

15 investigate [invéstəgèit]
v. 수사하다
▶ to ask questions and examine a situation in order to decide what is true
▶ investigation n. 수사, 조사

16 mock [mɑk]
v. 조롱하다
▶ to ridicule someone

17 satirical [sətírikəl]
a. 풍자의, 비꼬는
▶ criticizing something, mocking
▶ satire n. 풍자
▶ satirically ad. 풍자적으로

18 epidemic [èpədémik]
n. 유행병, 유행
▶ a particular disease that spreads very quickly

19 illustrate [íləstrèit]
v. 설명하다
▶ to explain; to let people understand
▶ illustration n. 설명

20 official [əfíʃəl]
n. 공무원, 관리 a. 관리의, 공식의
▶ a person who has authority in an organization
▶ officially ad. 공식적으로

21 life-long imprisonment [láiflɔ́:ŋ imprízənmənt]
종신형
▶ being put in prison for the rest of one's life

22 crawl [krɔ:l]
v. 기다, 아첨하다
▶ to move on hands and knees

23 vanish [vǽniʃ]
v. 사라지다
- ▶ to disappear; not to be seen

_____________   _____________

24 two-party system
[tuː pɑ́ːrti sístəm]
양당제
- ▶ a political system which consists of two different groups of politicians

_____________   _____________

25 minority [minɔ́ːriti]
n. 소수
- ▶ a number of people forming less than half in a larger group

_____________   _____________

26 handicapped [hǽndikæpt]
a. 장애를 가진
- ▶ having a physical or mental disability

_____________   _____________

27 racism [réisizəm]
n. 인종차별주의
- ▶ prejudice against an ethnic group; unfair treatment against a different race
- ▶ race n. 인종 a. 인종의, 인종적인
- ▶ racist n. 인종차별주의자

_____________   _____________

28 liberal [líbərəl]
a. 진보적인, 자유주의의
- ▶ progressive, broad-minded
- ▶ liberate v. 해방시키다
- ▶ liberty n. 해방, 자유
- ▶ liberalism n. 자유주의, 진보주의

_____________   _____________

29 conservative [kənsə́ːrvətiv]
a. 보수적인
- ▶ preserving the status, cautious
- ▶ conserve v. 보존하다
- ▶ conservation n. 보존
- ▶ conservatism n. 보수주의

_____________   _____________

Exercise

A 주어진 뜻에 해당하는 단어를 보기에서 찾아 쓰세요.

> requirement   trait   transparent   policy   bribery
> epidemic   official   two-party system   minority   conservative

① understandable, apparent, easily understood or recognized   ____________
② the act of giving money to people so that they will do what you want   ____________
③ preserving the status, cautious   ____________
④ a particular characteristic that someone has   ____________
⑤ a person who has authority in an organization   ____________
⑥ a political system which consists of two different groups of politicians   ____________
⑦ a set of plans used as a basis for an organization   ____________
⑧ a number of people forming less than half in a larger group   ____________
⑨ a particular disease that spreads very quickly   ____________
⑩ a quality or qualification that people need to have   ____________

B 단어의 관계에 맞게 빈칸을 채우세요.

① rigorous : rigor = 엄격한 : ________________
② courteous : courteously = 정중한 : ________________
③ corrupt : ________________ = 타락한 : 타락하기 쉬운
④ ________________ : resignation = 사임하다 : 사임
⑤ satirical : ________________ = 풍자의 : 풍자
⑥ illustrate : illustration = ________________ : 설명
⑦ racism : race = 인종차별주의 : ________________
⑧ liberal : ________________ = 자유주의의 : 해방시키다

C 의미가 같도록 알맞은 단어를 넣어 문장을 완성하세요.

1. What ________________ do they need?
   그들은 어떤 자격이 필요한 것일까?

2. During the interview, we should check carefully to see if they are ____________ .
   면접 중에 그들이 표리부동한 사람인지 세심하게 조사해야 해.

3. Grandpa said that people shouldn't have voted for those ____________ .
   할아버지께서는 사람들이 그 후보자들에게 투표하지 말았어야 했다고 말씀하셨어.

4. Are the police going to ________________ them thoroughly?
   경찰은 그들을 철저하게 수사할까?

5. In cyberspace, we can ________________ these people in funny ways.
   사이버 공간에서, 우리는 이 사람들을 재미있는 방법으로 조롱할 수 있어.

6. They have to ________________ around like bugs, making apologies.
   그들은 벌레처럼 기며 사죄를 해.

7. We can make them ________________ from our view.
   우리는 그들을 시야에서 사라지게 할 수도 있어.

8. They are sentenced to ________________ .
   그들은 종신형을 선고받아.

<table><tr><td>Date</td><td>Score</td></tr></table>

D 녹음된 내용을 듣고, 다음 빈칸에 들어갈 단어나 표현을 쓰세요.

Dear Sara,

What are __________ like? ● What are the __________ to enter parliament? ● What __________ do they need? ● People who want to become politicians should be given a __________ interview. ● During the interview, we should check carefully to see if they are __________. ● Many politicians seem to have some __________ in common. ● They pretend to be __________. ● They even promise voters that their actions will be __________. ● But, once they are elected, their __________ change. ● Recently, some politicians were involved in __________ scandals. ● Grandpa said that people shouldn't have voted for those __________. ● Their __________ actions are very serious. ● I think they should resign immediately. ● When will the __________ __________ intervene in these cases? ● Are the police going to __________ them thoroughly?

In cyberspace, we can __________ these people in funny ways. ● My friends like writing __________ jokes about them on their webpages. ● These things sweep through our country like an __________. ● They __________ how people feel about corrupt politicians. ● Sometimes government __________ at the highest rank are described as animals. ● They are sentenced to __________. ● They have to __________ around like bugs, making apologies. ● We can make them __________ from our view. ● If you're also interested in satirical games and jokes, please let me know.

Sara, I heard America has a __________ system, the Democrats and Republicans. ● Which party shows more support for the rights of __________ such as the __________? ● Are both parties strongly against __________? ● I heard the Democrats are more __________, while Republicans are more __________. ● Anyway, I hope both parties work for the people.●

Politics and Social Issues

▶ 1단계 : 먼저 그림을 보고, 이 장의 에피소드를 추측해 보세요.

→ **wear an electronic tag**

pros and cons about the punishment ←

→ **have to defend oneself**

Dear Diary,

Sara's story about the sex offender was horrible. ● How can he live wearing an electronic tag all his life? ● People can spot him so easily, so how can he get along with the other residents? ● What about his self-esteem? ● He might feel humiliated whenever people look at him. ● Then he may not be able to assimilate into his new neighborhood. ● There are some pros and cons about this punishment. ● It's such a controversial issue. ● Proponents say this punishment is effective. ● They argue that crime rates will fall. ● But opponents have some concerns about this type of punishment. ● Human rights activists are strongly against the idea.

This week the newspapers are full of stories about kidnapping. ● Two kids were found murdered after they were kidnapped. ● Most people are in a panic over these things and it provokes debate. ● The issue of the death penalty has come up again. ● Some people say public safety is our priority. ● I read some editorials in the papers, where many journalists expressed their opinions on these issues. ● I think the death penalty should be abolished.

Seri carries hair spray instead of perfume. ● She says she is going to use it if someone tries to harass her. ● She believes the spray emission will stop the person. ● Seri has always been brave when she confronts bullies. ● She never compromises when someone bullies her. ● She says she has to defend herself because her life is worth defending.

▶ **3단계 : 외우면서 단어를 2번씩 써보세요!**

1 sex offender [seks əféndər]
성범죄자
- ▶ a criminal who does crimes that involve sex or sexual behavior
- ▶ sex offence 성범죄

______________ ______________

2 electronic [ilèktránik]
a. 전자의
- ▶ involving the use of an electronic device
- ▶ electronics n. 전자공학
- ▶ electronically ad. 전자공학적으로

______________ ______________

3 resident [rézidənt]
n. 주민
- ▶ a person who lives in a particular area
- ▶ residential a. 주거의, 거주에 관한
- ▶ residentially ad. 거주지역에 관해

______________ ______________

4 self-esteem [self istí:m]
n. 자존심, 자부심
- ▶ how one feels about oneself

______________ ______________

5 humiliated [hju:mílièid]
a. 굴욕감을 느끼는, 창피한
- ▶ embarrassed and ashamed
- ▶ humiliate v. 굴욕감을 느끼게 하다
- ▶ humiliation n. 굴욕, 창피

______________ ______________

6 assimilate [əsíməlèit]
v. 동화되다
- ▶ to become adjusted, to blend in
- ▶ assimilation n. 동화

______________ ______________

7 pros and cons
[prás ænd káns]
찬반양론
- ▶ the good points (pros) and bad points (cons)

______________ ______________

▶ 외우면서 단어를 2번씩 써보세요!

8 controversial [kɑ̀ntrəvə́:rʃəl]
a. 논쟁의, 논란의 여지가 있는
▶ causing a lot of discussion and argument
▷ controversy n. 논란
▷ controversially ad. 논쟁적으로

9 proponent [prəpóunənt]
n. 찬성론자
▶ someone who supports an idea, opposite of opponent

10 crime [kraim]
n. 범죄
▶ an illegal action or activity
▷ criminal n. 범인

11 opponent [əpóunənt]
n. 반대론자
▶ someone who does not support an idea, opposite of proponent
▷ oppose v. 반대하다
▷ opposition n. 반대

12 human rights activist
[hjúːmən raits æktəvist]
인권 운동가
▶ someone who tries to protect other people who are underprivileged

13 kidnapping [kídnæper]
n. 유괴
▶ an act of taking someone away illegally and by force usually in order to get money
▷ kidnap v. 유괴하다, 납치하다
▷ kidnapper n. 유괴범

14 murder [mə́:rdər]
v. 살해하다 n. 살해
▶ to kill another person
▷ murderous a. 살인의, 살인적인

▶ 3단계 : 외우면서 단어를 2번씩 써보세요!

15 panic [pǽnik]
n. 돌연한 공포, 공황 a. 허둥대는
▶ extreme fright
▶ panicky a. 공포스러운
▶ in a panic 공포에 질린

16 provoke [prəvóuk]
v. 도발하다
▶ to cause something, to stimulate
▶ provocation n. 도발
▶ provocative a. 도발적인

17 death penalty [deθ pénəlti]
사형(제도)
▶ killing a criminal instead of putting them in prison

18 priority [praió(:)rəti]
n. 우선순위
▶ a thing that is more important than other things
▶ prioritize v. 우선순위를 매기다

19 editorial [èdətɔ́:riəl]
n. 사설
▶ a newspaper article written by an editor
▶ editorialize v. 사설로 논하다

20 journalist [dʒə́:rnəlist]
n. 언론인
▶ a person who reports or writes news stories for TV and newspapers
▶ journalism n. 언론
▶ journal n. 신문. 잡지

21 abolish [əbáliʃ]
v. 폐지하다
▶ to do away with a system or practice
▶ abolishment n. 폐지

▶ 외우면서 단어를 2번씩 써보세요!

22 perfume [pə́ːrfjuːm]
n. 향수 v. 향수를 뿌리다
▶ a nice smelling liquid
▶ perfumed a. 향수를 뿌린

23 harass [hǽrəs]
v. 괴롭히다, 귀찮게 굴다
▶ to annoy someone and make them angry
▶ harassment n. 괴롭힘, 희롱

24 emission [imíʃən]
n. 분사, 내뿜음
▶ the release of gas or liquid into the atmosphere
▶ emit v. 내뿜다, 분사하다

25 confront [kənfrʌ́nt]
v. 직면하다, 마주하다
▶ to encounter someone or something
▶ confrontation n. 직면, 대립

26 bully [búli]
v. 위협하다, 괴롭히다
n. 위협하는 사람
▶ to frighten someone

27 defend [difénd]
v. 방어하다
▶ to take action to protect someone or something
▶ defense n. 방어
▶ defensive a. 방어적인

28 worth [wə́ːrθ]
a. 가치가 있는 n. 가치, 중요성
▶ important enough for a particular action
▶ worthless a. 가치 없는
▶ be worth ~ing ~할 만한 가치가 있다

Exercise

A 주어진 뜻에 해당하는 단어를 보기에서 찾아 쓰세요.

> sex offender   assimilate   controversial   proponent   priority
> death penalty   journalist   editorial   harass   defend

① a thing that is more important than other things   _______________

② causing a lot of discussion and argument   _______________

③ to annoy someone and make them angry   _______________

④ killing a criminal instead of putting them in prison   _______________

⑤ to take action to protect someone or something   _______________

⑥ a criminal who does crimes that involve sex or sexual behavior   _______________

⑦ a newspaper article written by an editor   _______________

⑧ a person who reports or writes news stories for TV and newspapers   _______________

⑨ to become adjusted, to blend in   _______________

⑩ someone who supports an idea, opposite of opponent   _______________

B 단어의 관계에 맞게 빈칸을 채우세요.

① electronic : electronics = 전자의 : _______________

② resident : _______________ = 주민 : 주거의

③ crime : criminal = 범죄 : _______________

④ _______________ : oppose = 반대론자 : 반대하다

⑤ _______________ : provocation = 도발하다 : 도발

⑥ abolish : abolishment = _______________ : 폐지

⑦ confront : confrontation = _______________ : 직면

⑧ worth : _______________ = 가치 있는 : 가치 없는

C 의미가 같도록 알맞은 단어를 넣어 문장을 완성하세요.

1. He might feel _______________ whenever people look at him.
   사람들이 쳐다볼 때마다 그는 굴욕감을 느낄 텐데.

2. There are some _______________ about this punishment.
   이런 처벌에는 찬반양론이 있어.

3. This week the newspapers are full of stories about _______________ .
   이번 주 신문들은 유괴에 대한 기사로 가득해.

4. Two kids were found _______________ after they were kidnapped.
   어린이 두 명이 납치된 후에 살해되어 발견되었어.

5. Most people are in a _______________ over these things and it provokes debate.
   대부분의 사람들이 이것 때문에 공포에 떨게 되고, 그것이 논쟁을 유발시키고 있어.

6. Seri carries hair spray instead of _______________ .
   세리는 향수 대신 헤어 스프레이를 가지고 다녀.

7. She never compromises when someone _______________ her.
   그녀는 누군가 자신을 위협해도 절대 타협하지 않았어.

8. She believes the spray _______________ will stop the person.
   그녀는 스프레이 분사가 그 사람의 행동을 막아줄 것이라고 믿고 있어.

D 녹음된 내용을 듣고, 다음 빈칸에 들어갈 단어나 표현을 쓰세요. 

Dear Diary,

Sara's story about the ______________ ______________ was horrible. ● How can he live wearing an ______________ tag all his life? ● People can spot him so easily, so how can he get along with the other ______________? ● What about his ______________? ● He might feel ______________ whenever people look at him. ● Then he may not be able to ______________ into his new neighborhood. ● There are some ______________ ______________ ______________ about this punishment. ● It's such a ______________ issue. ● ______________ say this punishment is effective. ● They argue that ______________ rates will fall. ● But ______________ have some concerns about this type of punishment. ● ______________ ______________ ______________ are strongly against the idea.

This week the newspapers are full of stories about ______________. ● Two kids were found ______________ after they were kidnapped. ● Most people are in a ______________ over these things and it ______________ debate. ● The issue of the ______________ ______________ has come up again. ● Some people say public safety is our ______________. ● I read some ______________ in the papers, where many ______________ expressed their opinions on these issues. ● I think the death penalty should be ______________.

Seri carries hair spray instead of ______________. ● She says she is going to use it if someone tries to ______________ her. ● She believes the spray ______________ will stop the person. ● Seri has always been brave when she ______________ bullies. ● She never compromises when someone ______________ her. ● She says she has to ______________ herself because her life is ______________ defending.

Chapter 3

Politics and Social Issues

▶ 1단계 : 먼저 그림을 보고, 이 장의 에피소드를 추측해 보세요.

Dear Diary,

Hoony and his friend are playing computer games. ● They call each other the enemy. ● They each refer to themselves as a mighty army. ● They each have their own strategy. ● They dispatch warships. ● They also dispatch troops. ● Each has its own allies. ● They use many assault weapons. ● They attack each other by dropping atomic bombs. ● They try to occupy each other's territory. ● And the winner is the one who displaces his opponents. ● Finally, a message pops up, "Mission completed." ● Why do boys like such violent games? ● Hoony says it's not real, just imaginary. ● Recently, a war broke out in the Middle East. ● The authorities are meeting to make a treaty. ● When are they going to declare an end to war? ● Isn't it feasible? ● Why is it so hard to declare a cease-fire? ● One president said they started this war for justice. ● But both sides still blame each other. ● Innocent people are becoming refugees. ● They lack medicine and food. ● All their facilities are demolished. ● And their infrastructure has been destroyed. ● Some people say both sides fight over natural resources. ● Do the leaders even have a conscience? ● They even say in explicit terms that they want peace and justice. ● How can we ascertain their intentions? ● I doubt they think life is valuable.

▶ 3단계 : 외우면서 단어를 2번씩 써보세요!

1 enemy [énəmi]
n. 적
▶ someone who hates you and wants to argue or fight with you

2 mighty [máiti]
a. 강력한
▶ strong, powerful, hardy
▷ mightiness n. 위대, 강대

3 strategy [strǽtədʒi]
n. 전략
▶ a plan, an idea of the best way to do something
▷ strategize v. 전략을 짜다
▷ strategist n. 전략가
▷ strategic a. 전략의, 전략상 중요한

4 dispatch [dispǽtʃ]
v. 파견하다, 발송하다
▶ to send something to do a particular job or task

5 troop [truːp]
n. 군대
▶ a group of soldiers

6 ally [əlái]
n. 동맹국
▶ a country that supports another country and will fight its enemies
▷ alliance n. 동맹
▷ allied a. 연합된

7 assault [əsɔ́ːlt]
n. 공격 v. 공격하다
▶ a strong attack made by an army
▷ assault weapon 공격용 무기

▶ 외우면서 단어를 2번씩 써보세요!

8 atomic bomb [ətámik] [bɑml]
원자폭탄
▶ a bomb that causes an explosion by energy resulting from splitting atoms

9 occupy [ákjəpài]
v. 점령하다
▶ to take another person's land or country
▶ occupation n. 점령
▶ occupied a. 점령된

10 territory [térətɔ̀ːri]
n. 영토
▶ the area controlled by a particular country

11 displace [displéis]
v. 내쫓다, 내몰다
▶ to make people leave their land or country
▶ displacement n. 바꾸어 놓기, 퇴거

12 mission [míʃən]
n. 임무
▶ an important task or goal that one has to do
▶ missionary n. 선교사 a. 전도의

13 violent [váiələnt]
a. 폭력적인
▶ using physical force, destructive
▶ violence n. 폭력
▶ violently ad. 폭력적으로

14 imaginary [imædʒənèri]
a. 상상의, 가상의
▶ not real and only existing in one's mind
▶ imagination n. 상상
▶ imaginative a. 상상력이 풍부한

▶ 3단계 : 외우면서 단어를 2번씩 써보세요!

15 **break out** [breik aut]
발발하다, 일어나다
▶ to begin very quickly instead of over a long period of time

16 **treaty** [trí:ti]
n. 조약
▶ a contract that people write when they agree to make peace

17 **declare** [diklέər]
v. 선언하다
▶ to announce, to tell many people
▷ declaration n. 선언

18 **feasible** [fí:zəbəl]
a. 가능한, 있음직한
▶ possible, achievable
▷ feasibility n. 가능성, 타당성
▷ feasibly ad. 가능하게

19 **cease-fire** [si:s fáiər]
n. 정전, 휴전
▶ stop in fighting

20 **justice** [dʒʌ́stis]
n. 정의
▶ good and fair behavior towards other people
▷ justify v. 정당화하다
▷ justification n. 정당화

21 **blame** [bleim]
v. 비난하다, 탓하다
▶ to say that other people are wrong or a situation is someone else's fault

22 **refugee** [rèfjudʒí:]
n. 난민
▶ a person who has to leave their city or country because of war

▶ 외우면서 단어를 2번씩 써보세요!

23 lack [læk]
v. 부족하다 n. 부족, 결핍
▶ not to have enough of something
▶ lacking a. 부족한

24 demolish [dimáliʃ]
v. 파괴하다
▶ to destroy something; to smash something to pieces
▶ demolition n. 파괴, 폭파
▶ demolished a. 파괴된

25 infrastructure [ínfrəstrʌ̀ktʃər]
n. 기간시설
▶ the framework that allows a country to function, work and exist

26 resources [risɔ́ːrsiz]
n. 자원
▶ things such as food and materials that people can use to make things

27 conscience [kánʃəns]
n. 양심
▶ moral sense, a feeling of guilt
▶ conscientious a. 양심적인

28 explicit [iksplísit]
a. 분명한, 명백한
▶ expressed clearly and openly
▶ explicitly ad. 분명히, 분명하게

29 term [təːrm]
n. 용어
▶ a description of a concept, a word or expression

30 ascertain [æsərtéin]
v. 확인하다
▶ to make sure, to confirm
▶ ascertainment n. 확인
▶ ascertainable a. 확인할 수 있는

Exercise

A 주어진 뜻에 해당하는 단어를 보기에서 찾아 쓰세요.

> enemy　dispatch　ally　displace　treaty
> territory　declare　blame　demolish　infrastructure

① to make people leave their land or country ___________
② someone who hates you and wants to argue or fight with you ___________
③ to say that other people are wrong or a situation is someone else's fault ___________
④ the area controlled by a particular country ___________
⑤ the framework that allows a country to function, work and exist ___________
⑥ a country that supports another country and will fight its enemies ___________
⑦ to destroy something; to smash something to pieces ___________
⑧ a contract that people write when they agree to make peace ___________
⑨ to announce, to tell many people ___________
⑩ to send somethingto do a particular job or task ___________

B 단어의 관계에 맞게 빈칸을 채우세요.

① mighty : ___________ = 강력한 : 강대
② strategy : strategize = 전략 : ___________
③ occupy : ___________ = 점령하다 : 점령된
④ mission : missionary = 임무 : ___________
⑤ feasible : feasibly = 가능한 : ___________
⑥ justice : ___________ = 정의 : 정당화하다
⑦ ___________ : conscientious = 양심 : 양심적인
⑧ ascertain : ascertainable = 확인하다 : ___________

C 의미가 같도록 알맞은 단어를 넣어 문장을 완성하세요.

1. They also dispatch ___________ .
   그들은 군대도 파병해.

2. They use many ___________ weapons.
   그들은 많은 공격용 무기를 사용해.

3. Why do boys like such ___________ games?
   왜 남자아이들은 이런 폭력적인 게임을 좋아할까?

4. Recently, a war ___________ in the Middle East.
   최근에 중동에서 전쟁이 발발했어

5. Why is it so hard to declare a ___________ ?
   정전을 선언하는 것이 그렇게 어려울까?

6. Innocent people are becoming ___________ .
   선량한 사람들이 난민이 되어가고 있어.

7. Some people say both sides fight over natural ___________ .
   어떤 사람들은 양쪽이 천연자원을 놓고 싸운다고 말해.

8. They even say in ___________ terms that they want peace and justice.
   그들은 심지어 분명하게 그들이 평화와 정의를 원한다고 말해.

D 녹음된 내용을 듣고, 다음 빈칸에 들어갈 단어나 표현을 쓰세요.

Dear Diary,

Hoony and his friend are playing computer games. ● They call each other the __________. ● They each refer to themselves as a ______________ army. ● They each have their own __________. ● They ____________ warships. ● They also dispatch ________. ● Each has its own ____________. ● They use many __________ weapons. ● They attack each other by dropping __________ __________. ● They try to ________ each other's __________. ● And the winner is the one who ______________ his opponents. ● Finally, a message pops up, "__________ completed." ● Why do boys like such ____________ games? ● Hoony says it's not real, just _____________. ● Recently, a war ___________ out in the Middle East. ● The authorities are meeting to make a _____________. ● When are they going to ________ an end to war? ● Isn't it _________? ● Why is it so hard to declare a ____________? ● One president said they started this war for __________. ● But both sides still __________ each other. ● Innocent people are becoming __________. ● They _________ medicine and food. ● All their facilities are __________. ● And their ____________ has been destroyed. ● Some people say both sides fight over natural _____________. ● Do the leaders even have a __________? ● They even say in ___________ _________ that they want peace and justice. ● How can we ____________ their intentions? ● I doubt they think life is valuable.

Test (Unit 9~Unit 12)

Total

/ 30

■ 녹음을 듣고, 해당하는 단어와 뜻을 쓰세요.

1	단어:	뜻:	2	단어:	뜻:
3	단어:	뜻:	4	단어:	뜻:
5	단어:	뜻:	6	단어:	뜻:
7	단어:	뜻:	8	단어:	뜻:
9	단어:	뜻:	10	단어:	뜻:
11	단어:	뜻:	12	단어:	뜻:
13	단어:	뜻:	14	단어:	뜻:
15	단어:	뜻:	16	단어:	뜻:
17	단어:	뜻:	18	단어:	뜻:
19	단어:	뜻:	20	단어:	뜻:
21	단어:	뜻:	22	단어:	뜻:
23	단어:	뜻:	24	단어:	뜻:
25	단어:	뜻:	26	단어:	뜻:
27	단어:	뜻:	28	단어:	뜻:
29	단어:	뜻:	30	단어:	뜻:

접두사 sym-/syn- / uni-

sym-/syn-은 'together,' 'with'라는 뜻의 접두사로, '함께 또는 동시에 존재하다'는 뜻의 단어를 만든다. uni-는 'one'이라는 뜻의 접두사로, '유일한 또는 공동'이라는 뜻의 단어를 만든다.

sym-/syn-

-pathy 고통, 감정
sym + pathy = sympathy 공감, 동정
ex) My heart was filled with sympathy for the poor kid.
내 마음 속에 그 불쌍한 아이에 대한 동정심이 가득했다.

- **symphony** 교향곡, 연주회
- **symbiosis** 공생
- **symbiotic** 공생하는
- **synchronous** 동시에 일어나는
- **synchronize** 동시에 일어나다
- **synonym** 동의어
- **synthesis** 종합, 통합

uni-

-cycle 바퀴
uni + cycle = unicycle 외바퀴 자전거
ex) The clown on the unicycle waved to the audience.
외바퀴 자전거를 탄 광대가 관중을 향해 손을 흔들었다.

- **unicorn** 일각수
- **uniform** 한결같은, 동형의
- **unisex** 남녀 공용의
- **unilateral** 일면인, 일방적인
- **unify** 단일화하다
- **unicameral** 단원제의
- **unison** 동음, 화합

Culture Plus

U.S. Politics 미국 정치

+ the two-party system 양당제

+ the Republican Party 공화당

+ the Democratic Party 민주당

+ the Senate 상원

+ the House of Representatives 하원

+ primary election 예비 선거

+ ballot 투표 용지

Chapter 4   Economy

▶ 1단계 : 먼저 그림을 보고, 이 장의 에피소드를 추측해 보세요.

→ restrain consumer spending

use the subway to commute to work ←

→ have to be thrifty

Dear Diary,

The world's markets don't seem to be stable. ● And what does deflation mean? ● The newspaper says the unemployment rate keeps increasing. ● Entrepreneurs can't hire many employees. ● And some employees are being laid off. ● Companies say they are having financial difficulties. ● Why don't we ask the government to make an amendment to the laws to help them? ● Then the banks will have to comply with it. ● I mean, the bank can just print out abundant amounts of cash for all of us. ● But, some economists say that will just cause inflation. ● These days farmers are holding rallies downtown. ● They even burned their own agricultural products. ● Why do they protest? ● Are they expressing their anti-government sentiment? ● Farmers say that they are victims of globalization. ● They claim local products can't compete with imported goods because of their low prices. ● They demand that the government take some measures to help them. ● What if we were imposing heavy taxes on imported goods? ● I mean imposing a heavy import tariff. ● Oil prices have soared, too. ● These rising prices restrain consumer spending. ● The rising prices will bring the market into a deep recession. ● Dad will have to start using the subway to commute to work. ● The price of commodities is going up, too. ● Mom says we have to be thrifty. ● She intends to cut my allowance.

Mom: Bomi, the President is on TV saying we have to work hard to overcome this adversity.

Bomi: Mom, do you think your plan is adequate? ● What if I go bankrupt? ● I don't want to be in debt.

▶ **3단계 : 외우면서 단어를 2번씩 써보세요!**

1 stable [stéibl]
a. 안정된
▶ not easily moved or disturbed
▶ stabilize v. 안정화하다
▶ stability n. 안정. 안정성

2 deflation [difléiʃən]
n. 디플레이션
▶ a persistent decrease in the level of consumer prices
▶ deflate v. (가격, 통화를) 수축시키다. 수축하다

3 unemployment [ʌ̀nimplɔ́imənt]
n. 실업
▶ a condition of not having a job
▶ unemployed a. 실직한

4 entrepreneur [ɑ̀ːntrəprənə́ːr]
n. 기업가
▶ a person who runs his or her own business, a businessman
▶ entrepreneurship n. 기업 운영, 기업가 정신

5 lay off [léi ɔ́ːf]
정리해고하다
▶ to temporarily remove employees from working at a particular job

6 financial [finǽnʃəl]
a. 재정의, 금융의
▶ having to do with finance, money management, investments, etc.
▶ finance n. 금융. 재정

7 amendment [əméndmənt]
n. 개정, 수정
▶ a change made to a constitution or law
▶ amend v. 개정하다

▶ 외우면서 단어를 2번씩 써보세요!

⑧ comply [kəmplái]

v. 따르다, 준수하다

▶ to perform what someone has asked or ordered
▶ compliance n. (명령에 관한) 순응, 이행

⑨ abundant [əbʌ́ndənt]

a. 풍부한

▶ existing in plentiful amounts, affluent
▶ abound v. 많이 있다, 풍부하다
▶ abundance n. 풍부

⑩ inflation [infléiʃən]

n. 인플레이션

▶ a continuing rise in the general level of prices of goods and services
▶ inflate v. 팽창하다

⑪ rally [rǽli]

n. 집회 v. 규합하다, 단결하다

▶ a mass meeting intended to arouse group enthusiasm and support

⑫ agricultural [æ̀grikʌ́ltʃərəl]

a. 농업의

▶ having to do with or related to farming
▶ agriculture n. 농업

⑬ protest [prətést]

v. 항의하다 n. 항의

▶ to make a gesture or statement against something

⑭ sentiment [séntəmənt]

n. 감정

▶ an attitude based on one's thoughts and feelings, an idea or feeling expressed in words
▶ sentimental a. 감상적인, 감정적인

▶ **3단계 : 외우면서 단어를 2번씩 써보세요!**

⑮ globalization [glóubəlizéʃən]

n. 세계화

▶ the development of an increasingly global economy
▷ globalize v. 세계화하다
▷ global a. 세계적인

⑯ imported [impɔ́:rtid]

a. 수입된

▶ brought from a foreign country
▷ import v. 수입하다 n. 수입

⑰ take some measures
[teik sʌm méʒərz]

몇몇 조치를 취하다

▶ to take action in order to prevent something from happening

⑱ impose [impóuz]

v. 부과하다

▶ to establish or apply by authority
▷ imposition n. 부과
▷ impose A on B A를 B에 부과하다

⑲ tariff [tǽrif]

n. 관세

▶ a tax placed on imported goods

⑳ soar [sɔ:r]

v. 치솟다

▶ to ascend, to go higher and higher

㉑ restrain [ri:stréin]

v. 억제하다

▶ to prevent, to hold back, to make it difficult to do something
▷ restraint n. 억제, 제지

▶ 외우면서 단어를 2번씩 써보세요!

22 recession [riséʃən]
n. 침체, 불경기
▶ a period when the economy is doing badly
▶ recede v. 나빠지다, 후퇴하다

23 commute [kəmjúːt]
v. 통근하다 n. 통근, 통학
▶ to travel to work
▶ commuter n. 통근자 a. 통근(자)의

24 commodity [kəmádəti]
n. 상품
▶ a thing that is sold, goods

25 thrifty [θrífti]
a. 절약하는, 검소한
▶ being good at money management
▶ thrift n. 검약, 절약

26 intend [inténd]
v. 의도하다, 작정하다
▶ to have a purpose or goal in mind
▶ intention n. 의도, 작정

27 adversity [ædvə́ːrsəti]
n. 역경
▶ a state of serious or continued difficulties
▶ adverse a. 불리한, 반대의

28 adequate [ǽdikwit]
a. 적절한, 충분한
▶ acceptable, good enough, sufficient
▶ adequacy n. 적절함, 타당성

29 bankrupt [bǽŋkrʌpt]
a. 파산한
▶ being completely out of money, broke
▶ bankruptcy n. 파산

Exercise

A 주어진 뜻에 해당하는 단어를 보기에서 찾아 쓰세요.

> deflation   financial   comply   protest   soar
> restrain   recession   imported   rally   adequate

① to make a gesture or statement against something ________________
② a mass meeting intended to arouse group enthusiasm and support ________________
③ a persistent decrease in the level of consumer prices ________________
④ to prevent, to hold back, to make it difficult to do something ________________
⑤ a period when the economy is doing badly ________________
⑥ to perform what someone has asked or ordered ________________
⑦ acceptable, good enough, sufficient ________________
⑧ brought from a foreign country ________________
⑨ having to do with finance, money management, investments, etc. ________________
⑩ to ascend, to go higher and higher ________________

B 단어의 관계에 맞게 빈칸을 채우세요.

① unemployment : ________________ = 실업 : 실직한
② amendment : amend = 개정 : ________________
③ ________________ : agriculture = 농업의 : 농업
④ abundant : abound = 풍부한 : ________________
⑤ globalization : ________________ = 세계화 : 세계화하다
⑥ restrain : restraint = ________________ : 억제
⑦ thrifty : thrift = 절약하는 : ________________
⑧ bankrupt : ________________ = 파산한 : 파산

C 의미가 같도록 알맞은 단어를 넣어 문장을 완성하세요.

1. The world's markets don't seem to be ________________ .
   세계 시장이 안정적이지 못한 것 같아.

2. And some employees are being ________________ .
   어떤 직원들은 정리해고 당하고 있어.

3. But, some economists say that will just cause ________________ .
   그러나 어떤 경제학자들은 그것이 인플레이션만 유발시킬 것이라고 말해.

4. Are they expressing their anti-government ________________ ?
   그들은 자신들의 반정부 감정을 표출하는 걸까?

5. They demand that the government ________________ to help them.
   그들은 정부가 자신들을 도와줄 조치를 취해줄 것을 요구해.

6. What if we were ________________ heavy taxes on imported goods?
   우리가 수입품에 무거운 관세를 붙인다면 어떨까?

7. Dad will have to start using the subway to ________________ to work.
   아빠는 출퇴근할 때 지하철을 이용하셔야 할 거야.

8. She ________________ to cut my allowance.
   엄마는 내 용돈도 깎을 작정이야.

D 녹음된 내용을 듣고, 다음 빈칸에 들어갈 단어나 표현을 쓰세요.

Dear Diary,

The world's markets don't seem to be ___________. ● And what does ___________ mean? ● The newspaper says the ___________ rate keeps increasing. ● ___________ can't hire many employees. ● And some employees are being ___________. ● Companies say they are having ___________ difficulties. ● Why don't we ask the government to make an ___________ to the laws to help them? ● Then the banks will have to ___________ with it. ● I mean, the bank can just print out ___________ amounts of cash for all of us. ● But, some economists say that will just cause ___________. ● These days farmers are holding ___________ downtown. ● They even burned their own ___________ products. ● Why do they ___________? ● Are they expressing their anti-government ___________? ● Farmers say that they are victims of ___________. ● They claim local products can't compete with ___________ goods because of their low prices. ● They demand that the government ___________ ___________ to help them. ● What if we were ___________ heavy taxes on imported goods? ● I mean imposing a heavy import ___________. ● Oil prices have ___________, too. ● These rising prices ___________ consumer spending. ● The rising prices will bring the market into a deep ___________. ● Dad will have to start using the subway to ___________ to work. ● The price of ___________ is going up, too. ● Mom says we have to be ___________. ● She ___________ to cut my allowance.

....

Mom: Bomi, the President is on TV saying we have to work hard to overcome this ___________.

Bomi: Mom, do you think your plan is ___________? ● What if I go ___________? ● I don't want to be in debt.

Unit 14. Hoony is back from an economics camp.

Economy

▶ 1단계 : 먼저 그림을 보고, 이 장의 에피소드를 추측해 보세요.

→ **finish a course with honors**

→ **pretend to be a financial analyst**

Dear Diary,

Dad, what is today's stock index like? • "I think this particular item is undervalued," says Hoony. • He is just quoting comments by an expert. • Hoony received his certificate from an economics camp. • He is boasting that he finished the course with honors. • He really cherishes his certificate. • "What's this graph for?" I asked Hoony. • Presumably, he is trying to figure out some basic principles of economics. • He keeps saying people's desires are infinite while resources are finite. • Hoony is talking like a scholar. • He pretends to have gained a profound knowledge of economics. • He also likes pretending to be a financial analyst.

Hoony: Dad, is animation a prosperous business? • I learned at the camp that the prospects of success for a business are important. • And are we insured against fire?

D a d : No, but we have car insurance.

Hoony: Dad, where is the warranty of my new computer CD?

D a d : In the drawer, I guess.

B o m i : Hoony, can you help with my investment plans?

Hoony: Sure. Why don't you deposit more money in the bank? • Or why don't you invest money in real estate?

I have approximately 50,000 won in my bank account. • About 20 won worth of interest has been added. • If interest is added at these amounts, when can I accumulate a fortune and become a millionaire?

▶ 3단계 : 외우면서 단어를 2번씩 써보세요!

1 stock index [stɑk índeks]
주가지수
▶ a measure of the current values of stock in a market

2 undervalue [Ὰndərvǽljuː]
v. 저평가하다
▶ to treat something as having less value than it does
▶ undervalued a. 저평가된

3 quote [kwout]
v. 인용하다
n. 인용문
▶ to speak or write something already stated by another person
▶ quotation n. 인용

4 certificate [sərtífəkit]
n. 수료증, 증명서
v. 증명하다
▶ a document stating that someone has made certain accomplishments
▶ certify v. (서명 날인한 문서로) 증명하다. 인증하다

5 with honors [wið ánərz]
우등으로
▶ with extremely high scores, at a high level, worthy of honorary status

6 cherish [tʃériʃ]
v. 소중히 여기다
▶ to hold dear, to feel affection for, to care about deeply

7 graph [græf]

n. 그래프, 도표
v. 그래프로 나타내다

▶ a diagram or chart used for measuring the differences among things

8 presumably [prizú:məbli]

ad. 아마도

▶ likely, reasonably, by reasonable assumption
▶ presume v. 추정하다
▶ presumption n. 추정

9 infinite [ínfənit]

a. 무한한

▶ unending, eternal, something that goes on forever
▶ infinity n. 무한

10 finite [fáinait]

a. 제한된

▶ limited

11 scholar [skálər]

n. 학자

▶ an academic person who is very involved in learning
▶ scholarly a. 학자의, 학자다운

12 profound [prəfáund]

a. 심오한, 깊이 있는

▶ intellectual, deep

13 analyst [ǽnəlist]

n. 분석가

▶ a person who examines and determines, an examiner
▶ analyze v. 분석하다
▶ analysis n. 분석

14 prosperous [práspərəs]
a. 번영하는, 성공한
▶ affluent, booming, successful, thriving
▶ prosper v. 번영하다
▶ prosperity n. 번영, 번창

15 prospect [práspekt]
n. 가능성, 전망
▶ an outlook on the future
▶ prospective a. 예상된, 가망 있는

16 insured [inʃúərd]
a. 보험에 든
▶ safeguarded, protected against
▶ insure v. 보험에 들다

17 insurance [inʃúərəns]
n. 보험
▶ security allowance

18 warranty [wɔ́(ː)rənti]
n. 품질보증서
▶ an assurance of security, a promise of replacement for broken products

19 investment [invéstmənt]
n. 투자
▶ money given with an expectation of more money received later
▶ invest v. 투자하다
▶ investor n. 투자자

▶ 외우면서 단어를 2번씩 써보세요!

20 deposit [dipázit]

v. 예치하다 n. 예치

▶ to put money into a bank account

__________ __________

21 real estate [ríːəl istéit]

부동산

▶ property in the form of land and buildings

__________ __________

22 approximately [əpráksəmitli]

ad. 대략

▶ about, nearly, around

__________ __________

23 interest [íntərist]

n. 이자

▶ money earned on an investment or deposit

__________ __________

24 accumulate [əkjúːmjəlèit]

v. 모으다, 축척하다

▶ to collect or gather something
▶ accumulation n. 축척

__________ __________

25 millionaire [mìljənɛ́ər]

n. 백만장자

▶ a person with more than one million dollars

__________ __________

Exercise

A 주어진 뜻에 해당하는 단어를 보기에서 찾아 쓰세요.

> cherish   graph   stock index   presumably   scholar
> analyst   insured   millionaire   interest   with honors

① likely, reasonably, by reasonable assumption   _______________
② to hold dear, to feel affection for, to care about deeply   _______________
③ a person who examines and determines, an examiner   _______________
④ a person with more than one million dollars   _______________
⑤ a measure of the current values of stock in a market   _______________
⑥ money earned on an investment or deposit   _______________
⑦ a diagram or chart used for measuring the differences among things   _______________
⑧ safeguarded, protected against   _______________
⑨ with extremely high scores, at a high level, worthy of honorary status   _______________
⑩ an academic person who is very involved in learning   _______________

B 단어의 관계에 맞게 빈칸을 채우세요.

① quote : _________________ = 인용하다 : 인용
② undervalue : undervalued = 저평가하다 : _________________
③ presumably : presume = 아마도 : _________________
④ _________________ : infinity = 무한한 : 무한
⑤ prospect : _________________ = 가능성 : 가망 있는
⑥ investment : investor = 투자 : _________________
⑦ accumulate : accumulation = 모으다 : _________________
⑧ _________________ : prosper = 번영하는 : 번영하다

C 의미가 같도록 알맞은 단어를 넣어 문장을 완성하세요.

1. Hoony received his _________________ from an economics camp.
   후니는 경제캠프에서 수료증을 받았어.

2. "I think this particular item is _________________ ," says Hoony.
   "이 품목이 가치가 저평가된 것 같아요"라고 후니가 말해.

3. He keeps saying people's desires are infinite while resources are ___________ .
   그는 자원은 제한되어 있는데 인간의 욕망은 끝이 없다는 말을 계속해서 해.

4. He pretends to have gained a _________________ knowledge of economics.
   그는 경제학에 대해 심오한 지식을 얻은 척해.

5. Dad, where is the _________________ of my new computer CD?
   아빠, 새로 산 컴퓨터 CD의 품질보증서 어디 있어요?

6. No, but we have car _________________ .
   아니, 하지만 자동차 보험은 있단다.

7. Sure. Why don't you _________________ more money in the bank?
   물론. 은행에 더 많은 돈을 예치하지 그래?

8. Or why don't you invest money in _________________ ?
   아니면 부동산에 투자하는 게 어때?

D 녹음된 내용을 듣고, 다음 빈칸에 들어갈 단어나 표현을 쓰세요.

Dear Diary,

Dad, what is today's _____________________ like? ● "I think this particular item is _______________," says Hoony. ● He is just _________ comments by an expert. ● Hoony received his _________ from an economics camp. ● He is boasting that he finished the course _________ _________. ● He really _________ his certificate. ● "What's this _________ for?" I asked Hoony. ● _________, he is trying to figure out some basic principles of economics. ● He keeps saying people's desires are _______ while resources are ___________. ● Hoony is talking like a _________. ● He pretends to have gained a ___________ knowledge of economics. ● He also likes pretending to be a financial ____________.

Hoony: Dad, is animation a ___________ business? ● I learned at the camp that the _____________ of success for a business are important. ● And are we ___________ against fire?

D a d : No, but we have car ___________.

Hoony: Dad, where is the ___________ of my new computer CD?

D a d : In the drawer, I guess.

B o m i : Hoony, can you help with my ___________ plans?

Hoony: Sure. Why don't you _____________ more money in the bank? ● Or why don't you invest money in _______ _________?

I have _____________ 50,000 won in my bank account. ● About 20 won worth of _________ has been added. ● If interest is added at these amounts, when can I _________ a fortune and become a _________?

Chapter 4 — Economy

Economy

▶ 1단계 : 먼저 그림을 보고, 이 장의 에피소드를 추측해 보세요.

→ **read how to transplant**

be replaced by modernized buildings ←

→ **transform the landscape**

Dear Sara,

Sara, how many people do you think live in the Seoul metropolitan area? • Our sociology teacher said about a quarter of the whole population dwells here. • I also learned that a lot of people migrate here from rural areas. • Now I can understand why dad complains that the subway is overcrowded. • He isn't satisfied with the quality of life in Seoul. • He sometimes says he will leave Seoul after retirement. • He says he will buy a few acres of land in a remote area. • Like a botanist, he reads books on growing plants. • He read a book about growing organic fruit. • And he is reading how to transplant grape trees. • I don't know if he can discern which grapes are ripe. • Does he know what to do to increase his yield? • Can mom adapt to farming?

Bomi: Where is the vacant lot where you were playing with Kite?
Hoony: It's gone. It has become a construction site.

Construction must be a thriving business. • It has been booming. • The blueprint of our neighborhood is changing rapidly. • Most old houses have been replaced by modernized buildings. • Apartment buildings are multiplying. • It's like new buildings are just being replicated, transforming the landscape. • Our neighborhood has altered a lot since Sara left. • Hoony and Kite used to play in that empty space. • Now it is restricted to construction workers. • My mom expects the land price to go up. • But Hoony and Kite miss their playground.

▶ 3단계 : 외우면서 단어를 2번씩 써보세요!

1 metropolitan
[mètrəpálitən]
a. 수도의, 대도시의
▶ urban, main area of a city
▶ metropolis n. 주요 도시, 대도시

2 dwell [dwel]
v. 거주하다
▶ to live in or at, to reside
▶ dwelling n. 거주

3 migrate [máigreit]
v. 이주하다
▶ to move, to emigrate or immigrate
▶ migration n. 이주
▶ migratory a. 이주하는, 이주성의

4 overcrowded
[òuvərkráudid]
a. 만원인
▶ jammed, packed, having too many people

5 quality [kwáləti]
n. 질, 품질
a. 훌륭한

6 retirement [ritáiərmənt]
n. 은퇴, 퇴직
▶ leaving one's job and usually stopping working completely
▶ retire v. 은퇴하다

7 acre [éikər]
n. 에이커
▶ a piece of land, a measure of an area of land

8 botanist [bátənist]
n. 식물학자
▶ a person who studies plants
▷ botany n. 식물학

9 organic [ɔːrgǽnik]
a. 유기농의
▶ not using chemicals in growing animals or plants

10 transplant [trænsplǽnt]
v. 이식하다 n. 이식
▶ to relocate, to move from one location to another
▷ transplanter n. 이식자
▷ transplantation n. 이식

11 discern [disə́ːrn]
v. 구별하다
▶ to recognize and understand something
▷ discernment n. 구별, 식별

12 ripe [raip]
a. 익은
▶ fully developed, ready to be picked
▷ ripen v. 익다, 익히다

13 yield [jiːld]
n. 소출, 수확
v. 산출하다
▶ product of labor, amount of crops produced

14 adapt [ədǽpt]
v. 적응하다
▶ to change or adjust to a different situation
▷ adaptability n. 적응성, 순응성
▷ adaptation n. 적응, 개조
▷ adaptable a. 적응할 수 있는, 융통성 있는
▷ adapt to ~에 적응하다

▶ **3단계 : 외우면서 단어를 2번씩 써보세요!**

15 vacant [véikənt]

a. 비어 있는

▶ empty, unoccupied, abandoned
▶ vacate v. 비우다
▶ vacancy n. 공허, 빈터

16 construction [kənstrʌ́kʃən]

n. 건설, 건축

▶ building, a creation of new buildings
▶ construct v. 건설하다
▶ constructive a. 건설적인

17 thriving [θráiviŋ]

a. 번창하는, 성공하는

▶ successful, prosperous, flourishing
▶ thrive v. 번창하다

18 booming [bú:miŋ]

a. 급속히 발전하는

▶ improving, growing or succeeding steadily
▶ boom v. 경기가 좋아지다 n. 성황, 인기

19 blueprint [blú:prìnt]

n. 청사진, 계획

▶ an architectural plan; a project

20 modernized [mádərnàizd]

a. 현대화된

▶ improved, up to date, remodeled
▶ modernize v. 현대화하다
▶ modernization n. 현대화

▶ 외우면서 단어를 2번씩 써보세요!

21 multiply [mʌ́ltəplài]

v. 늘다, 증가하다

▶ to increase, to reproduce
▶ multiplication n. 증가, 배가

22 replicate [répləkèit]

v. 복제하다

▶ to duplicate, to reproduce
▶ replication n. 복제, 모사
▶ replicated a. 복제된

23 transform [trænsfɔ́ːrm]

v. 변형시키다

▶ to change completely, to alter
▶ transformation n. 변형
▶ transformative a. 변형시키는, 변형의

24 alter [ɔ́ːltər]

v. 달라지다, 바꾸다

▶ to change, to adjust
▶ alteration n. 변경

25 restricted [ristríktid]

a. 제한된

▶ allowed to only people with special permission; limited
▶ restrict v. 제한하다
▶ restriction n. 제한

26 land price [lænd prais]

땅값

▶ the cost of a piece of land

Exercise

A 주어진 뜻에 해당하는 단어를 보기에서 찾아 쓰세요.

> overcrowded   migrate   acre   organic   transplant
> thriving   booming   replicate   restricted   modernized

① improving, growing or succeeding steadily   ____________
② jammed, packed, having too many people   ____________
③ successful, prosperous, flourishing   ____________
④ allowed to only people with special permission; limited   ____________
⑤ not using chemicals in growing animals or plants   ____________
⑥ to duplicate, to reproduce   ____________
⑦ to relocate, to move from one location to another   ____________
⑧ improved, up to date, remodeled   ____________
⑨ to move, to emigrate or immigrate   ____________
⑩ a piece of land, a measure of an area of land   ____________

B 단어의 관계에 맞게 빈칸을 채우세요.

① _______________ : metropolis = 대도시의 : 대도시
② dwell : _______________ = 거주하다 : 거주
③ botanist : botany = 식물학자 : _______________
④ ripe : ripen = 익은 : _______________
⑤ adapt : _______________ = 적응하다 : 적응성
⑥ vacant : _______________ = 비어 있는 : 공허, 빈터
⑦ alter : alteration = _______________ : 변경
⑧ _______________ : multiplication = 늘다 : 증가

C 의미가 같도록 알맞은 단어를 넣어 문장을 완성하세요.

1. He isn't satisfied with the _______________ of life in Seoul.
   그는 서울에서의 삶의 질에 만족하지 못하셔.

2. He sometimes says he will leave Seoul after _______________ .
   그는 은퇴하면 서울을 떠나시겠다고 가끔 말씀하셔.

3. I don't know if he can _______________ which grapes are ripe.
   나는 그가 어느 포도가 익었는지 구별하실지 모르겠어.

4. Does he know what to do to increase his _______________ ?
   그는 수확을 늘리기 위해 무엇을 해야 할지 아실까?

5. It's gone. It has become a _______________ site.
   없어졌어. 지금은 공사 부지가 되어버렸어.

6. The _______________ of our neighborhood is changing rapidly.
   우리 동네 청사진이 빠르게 바뀌고 있다.

7. It's like new buildings are just being replicated, __________ the landscape.
   그것은 마치 새로운 건물들이 주변의 모습을 바꾸면서 계속 복제되는 것만 같다.

8. My mom expects the _______________ to go up.
   우리 엄마는 땅값이 오르기를 기대하신다.

D 녹음된 내용을 듣고, 다음 빈칸에 들어갈 단어나 표현을 쓰세요.

Dear Sara,

Sara, how many people do you think live in the Seoul ____________ area? ● Our sociology teacher said about a quarter of the whole population _________ here. ● I also learned that a lot of people __________ here from rural areas. ● Now I can understand why dad complains that the subway is ______________. ● He isn't satisfied with the __________ of life in Seoul. ● He sometimes says he will leave Seoul after __________. ● He says he will buy a few _________ of land in a remote area. ● Like a __________, he reads books on growing plants. ● He read a book about growing _________ fruit. ● And he is reading how to _________ grape trees. ● I don't know if he can __________ which grapes are ripe. ● Does he know what to do to increase his __________? ● Can mom _______ to farming?

B o m i : Where is the ________ lot where you were playing with Kite?

Hoony: It's gone. It has become a ____________ site.

Construction must be a __________ business. ● It has been ___________. ● The _________ of our neighborhood is changing rapidly. ● Most old houses have been replaced by __________ buildings. ● Apartment buildings are __________. ● It's like new buildings are just being __________, ______________ the landscape. ● Our neighborhood has _________ a lot since Sara left. ● Hoony and Kite used to play in that empty space. ● Now it is __________ to construction workers. ● My mom expects the __________ to go up. ● But Hoony and Kite miss their playground.

Total
/ 30

■ 녹음을 듣고, 해당하는 단어와 뜻을 쓰세요.

1	단어:	뜻:	2	단어:	뜻:
3	단어:	뜻:	4	단어:	뜻:
5	단어:	뜻:	6	단어:	뜻:
7	단어:	뜻:	8	단어:	뜻:
9	단어:	뜻:	10	단어:	뜻:
11	단어:	뜻:	12	단어:	뜻:
13	단어:	뜻:	14	단어:	뜻:
15	단어:	뜻:	16	단어:	뜻:
17	단어:	뜻:	18	단어:	뜻:
19	단어:	뜻:	20	단어:	뜻:
21	단어:	뜻:	22	단어:	뜻:
23	단어:	뜻:	24	단어:	뜻:
25	단어:	뜻:	26	단어:	뜻:
27	단어:	뜻:	28	단어:	뜻:
29	단어:	뜻:	30	단어:	뜻:

Voca Plus

trans-는 'across'라는 뜻의 접두사로,'넘거나 가로지르다'라는 뜻의 단어를 만든다.
sur-는 'over'라는 뜻의 접두사로,'어떤 기준 이상'이라는 뜻의 단어를 만든다.

trans-

portare 들다
trans + port = transport 운송하다
ex) Your mission is to secretly transport the documents to his office.
당신의 임무는 비밀리에 서류를 그의 사무실까지 운반하는 것이다.

- **transplant** 이식하다
- **transcribe** 베끼다
- **transform** 변형시키다
- **transcontinental** 대륙 저편의
- **transpolar** 극지를 넘는
- **transparent** 투명한
- **transparency** 투명함

sur-

pass 지나가다
sur + pass = surpass 능가하다
ex) The experience surpassed my wildest dreams.
그 경험은 나의 가장 극단적인 상상을 초월했다.

- **surplus** 나머지, 잔여
- **surcharge** 추가 요금
- **surmount** 넘어 오르다, 극복하다
- **surface** 표면
- **surreal** 비현실의
- **surtax** 부가세
- **survive** 살아남다

Culture Plus

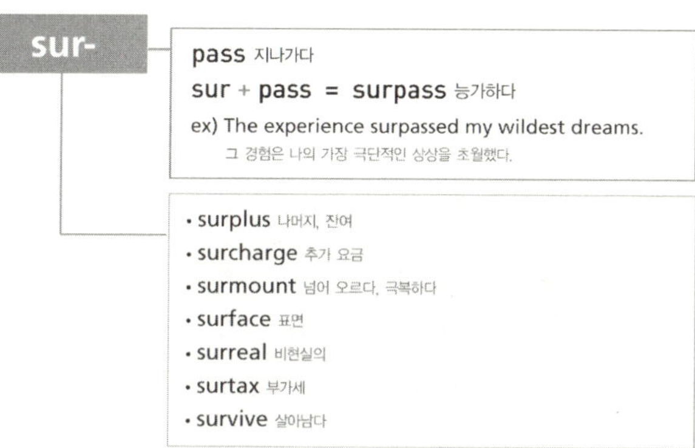

Investments 투자

+ **financial products** 금융 상품

+ **stocks** 주식

+ **bonds** 채권

+ **trust fund** 신탁 자금

+ **securities** 유가 증권

+ **high risk** 고위험

+ **high return** 고수익

SMART

Level.6

VOCA EDGE

Technology

Chapter 5

Technology

Unit 16. How amazing our life has become!

▶ 1단계 : 먼저 그림을 보고, 이 장의 에피소드를 추측해 보세요.

→ **have video conferences**

● **pay utilities by using Internet banking** ←

→ **become three-dimensional**

●**be converted into an interactive display** ←

Dear Diary,

High-tech products can be applied in various ways. • Because of our new technology, location and time are no longer barriers. • It has brought about drastic changes in our lives. • It really enables us to experience things that were inconceivable in the past. • My dad doesn't have to go abroad to have international conferences. • Once a week he has video conferences instead of conventional meetings. • He can talk with clients anywhere in the world at any time. • If our ancestors came to life, they would call our technology revolutionary.

Diary, my mom is never early to adopt new technology. • She prefers her analog watch to a digital one. • A few months ago, she didn't use the Internet banking services. • She was worried that they would malfunction. • But after she paid our utilities by using Internet banking, she realized how convenient it was. • Now, every month she transfers my allowance into my bank account. • She even transmits photos to my grandparents via the Internet.

Sara emailed me about an interesting museum. • If you touch art pieces, they are instantly converted into interactive displays. • When she touched the paintings, the subjects in the paintings danced and even answered her questions. • For example, *The Mona Lisa*, by Leonardo da Vinci, talked about the lives of aristocrats during the 15th century. • *Mona Lisa* also explained their unique customs. • She said that drawing portraits was in fashion during those days.

Diary, can you conceive of a huge 10 dollar bill about the size of a house? • Sounds weird, doesn't it? • But try to imagine a specimen of a 10 dollar bill multiplied in size by 100 times. • When Sara touched a part of the bill, it became three-dimensional. • Interestingly, a referee appeared on the screen and threw a ball to her. • I'm curious who devised this system. • The graphics are really amazing.

▶ **3단계 : 외우면서 단어를 2번씩 써보세요!**

1 high-tech [hai tek]
a. 첨단 기술의
▶ the newest and most advanced

2 barrier [bǽriər]
n. 장애
▶ something that stops one from doing something, an obstacle

3 drastic [drǽstik]
a. 엄청난, 격렬한
▶ severe, extreme and sudden
▷ drastically ad. 엄청나게, 격렬하게

4 inconceivable [ìnkənsí:vəbəl]
a. 상상할 수 없는
▶ difficult to believe, very unlikely to happen or be true
▷ inconceivably ad. 상상할 수 없게

5 conference [kάnfərəns]
n. 회의
▶ a formal meeting

6 conventional [kənvénʃənəl]
a. 전통적인, 재래식의
▶ normal, traditional
▷ convention n. 관습, 풍습
▷ conventionally ad. 전통적으로, 의례적으로

7 client [klάiənt]
n. 고객
▶ a customer or a person who one does business with

▶ 외우면서 단어를 2번씩 써보세요!

⑧ revolutionary [rèvəlúːʃənèri]

a. 혁신적인

▶ innovative, progressive
▶ revolution n. 혁명

_______________ _______________

⑨ adopt [ədápt]

v. 채택하다, 양자로 삼다

▶ to take something; to accept something
▶ adoption n. 채택, 입양

_______________ _______________

⑩ analog watch [ǽnəlòːg wɑtʃ]

아날로그 시계

▶ a watch that uses pointers that move around a dial, opposite of digital watch

_______________ _______________

⑪ Internet banking [íntərnèt bǽŋkiŋ]

인터넷뱅킹

▶ doing your banking by using the Internet

_______________ _______________

⑫ malfunction [mælfʌ́ŋkʃən]

v. 제대로 작동하지 않다
n. 고장

▶ not to work properly

_______________ _______________

⑬ utility [juːtíləti]

n. 공공 설비

▶ an important service such as electricity, gas and water

_______________ _______________

⑭ transfer [trænsfə́ːr]

v. 송금하다, 전달하나

▶ to move something from one location to another
▶ transference n. 이동, 전송

_______________ _______________

▶ 3단계 : 외우면서 단어를 2번씩 써보세요!

15 transmit [trænsmít]

v. 전송하다

▶ to send something by using a computer or electronic device
▶ transmission n. 전송

16 convert [kənvə́:rt]

v. 변하게 하다, 전환하다

▶ to change something into a different form
▶ conversion n. 전환

17 interactive [ìntərǽktiv]

a. 상호작용을 하는

▶ allowing people to be involved with something
▶ interact v. 상호작용하다
▶ interaction n. 상호작용

18 subject [sʌ́bdʒikt]

n. 피사체, 대상

▶ a person or object in a painting

19 aristocrat [ərístəkræt]

n. 귀족

▶ a person of high status, for example a duchess or marquis
▶ aristocracy n. 귀족정치
▶ aristocratic a. 귀족의

20 unique [ju:ní:k]

a. 독특한

▶ very unusual and special
▶ uniqueness n. 독특함

21 portrait [pɔ́:rtrit]

n. 초상화

▶ a picture of a person's face
▶ portray v. (초상을) 그리다
▶ portraiture n. 초상화법
▶ portrayal n. 그리기, 묘사

▶ 외우면서 단어를 2번씩 써보세요!

22 conceive [kənsíːv]

v. 상상하다

▶ to imagine
▶ conceivable a. 상상할 수 있는

_________________ _________________

23 weird [wiərd]

a. 이상한

▶ strange and peculiar

_________________ _________________

24 specimen [spésəmən]

n. 견본

▶ one example of an object, a sample

_________________ _________________

25 three-dimensional [θriːdiménʃənəl]

a. 입체적인

▶ having depth instead of looking like a flat picture

_________________ _________________

26 referee [réfəríː]

n. 심판 v. 심판하다

▶ a person who controls the players in a sports match

_________________ _________________

27 devise [diváiz]

v. 고안하다, 발명하다

▶ to make something, to invent something
▶ device n. 장치

_________________ _________________

28 graphics [grǽfiks]

n. 그래픽

▶ pictures - usually created on a computer

_________________ _________________

Exercise

A 주어진 뜻에 해당하는 단어를 보기에서 찾아 쓰세요.

> barrier   inconceivable   utility   revolutionary   analog watch
> interactive   subject   weird   specimen   referee

① at uses pointers that move around a dial, opposite of digital watch ________________
② an important service such as electricity, gas and water ________________
③ a person or object in a painting ________________
④ difficult to believe, very unlikely to happen or be true ________________
⑤ one example of an object, a sample ________________
⑥ allowing people to be involved with something ________________
⑦ strange and peculiar ________________
⑧ something that stops one from doing something, an obstacle ________________
⑨ a person who controls the players in a sports match ________________
⑩ innovative, progressive ________________

B 단어의 관계에 맞게 빈칸을 채우세요.

① drastic : drastically = ________________ : 엄청나게
② conventional : ________________ = 전통적인 : 관습
③ ________________ : adoption = 채택하다 : 채택
④ transfer : transference = 전달하다 : ________________
⑤ aristocrat : aristocracy = 귀족 : ________________
⑥ unique : ________________ = 독특한 : 독특함
⑦ portrait : ________________ = 초상화 : 그리기, 묘사
⑧ conceive : conceivable = 상상하다 : ________________

C 의미가 같도록 알맞은 단어를 넣어 문장을 완성하세요.

1. My dad doesn't have to go abroad to have international ________________ .
   우리 아빠는 국제 회의를 하기 위해 해외로 가실 필요가 없어.

2. He can talk with ________________ anywhere in the world at any time.
   어느 때든지 세계 어디에 있는 고객들과도 이야기를 할 수 있어.

3. A few months ago, she didn't use the ________________ services.
   몇 달 전에, 그녀는 인터넷뱅킹 서비스를 사용하지 않으셨어.

4. She was worried that they would ________________ .
   그녀는 제대로 되지 않을 것이라고 걱정하셨던 거야.

5. She even ________________ photos to my grandparents via the Internet.
   그녀는 인터넷으로 우리 조부모님께 사진도 전송하셔.

6. If you touch art pieces, they are instantly ________________ into interactive displays.
   만일 미술 작품을 만지면, 즉시 상호작용이 가능한 작품으로 변해.

7. When Sara touched a part of the bill, it became ________________.
   사라가 그 지폐의 일부분에 손을 댔을 때, 그것은 입체적이 되었어.

8. I'm curious who ________________ this system.
   나는 이 시스템을 누가 생각해냈는지 궁금해.

D 녹음된 내용을 듣고, 다음 빈칸에 들어갈 단어나 표현을 쓰세요.

Dear Diary,

_____________ products can be applied in various ways. ● Because of our new technology, location and time are no longer _________. ● It has brought about _________ changes in our lives. ● It really enables us to experience things that were _____________ in the past. ● My dad doesn't have to go abroad to have international conferences. ● Once a week he has video conferences instead of _____________ meetings. ● He can talk with ___________ anywhere in the world at any time. ● If our ancestors came to life, they would call our technology _____________.

Diary, my mom is never early to _________ new technology. ● She prefers her _________ to a digital one. ● A few months ago, she didn't use the _________ _______ services. ● She was worried that they would _________. ● But after she paid our ________ by using Internet banking, she realized how convenient it was. ● Now, every month she _________ my allowance into my bank account. ● She even _____________ to my grandparents via the Internet.

Sara emailed me about an interesting museum. ● If you touch art pieces, they are instantly ___________ into ___________ displays. ● When she touched the paintings, the ________ in the paintings danced and even answered her questions. ● For example, *The Mona Lisa*, by Leonardo da Vinci, talked about the lives of _________ during the 15th century. ● *Mona Lisa* also explained their ________ customs. ● She said that drawing _________ was in fashion during those days.

Diary, can you _________ of a huge 10 dollar bill about the size of a house? ● Sounds _________, doesn't it? ● But try to imagine a _________ of a 10 dollar bill multiplied in size by 100 times. ● When Sara touched a part of the bill, it became _____________. ● Interestingly, a ___________ appeared on the screen and threw a ball to her. ● I'm curious who _________ this system. ● The _________ are really amazing.●

▶ 1단계 : 먼저 그림을 보고, 이 장의 에피소드를 추측해 보세요.

→ **update one's own blog with music and photos** ●

→ **infringe on one's copyright** ○

Dear Diary,

Blogging is an outlet for my creative ideas. • For a few weeks, I updated my own blog with music and photos. • I downloaded music and the Volcanoes' photos. • Then I paired the two components, music and photos. • Sometimes I matched classical music with the Volcanoes' photos. • I spent a few hours combining the best pairs. • The results were phenomenal. • Every day over 400 people visited my blog. • They left quite positive and complimentary messages. • Someone wrote that my materials were ingenious. • I was delighted to read the messages. • It was gratifying to entertain others. • Today I found a warning message. • Some music files had been deleted. • I was very confused. • There was a written message, "You're not allowed to use these materials."

Bomi: What's wrong? • Am I going to be arrested by cybercops? • Are there any defects in my materials? • Mom, why do they think my materials are illegal?

Mom: It's related to copyright laws.

Bomi: But I didn't utilize the materials for anything other than my personal interest.

Mom: Other people's creations should be treated like personal property. • If you used the materials without the owner's permission, it's like theft. • If someone asserts copyright properties of their materials, you have to give it back to them. • The owner may try to sue you for money.

Bomi: I didn't know I was infringing on their copyright. • From now on, I'll obtain their consent before I use someone else's materials.

1. outlet [áutlet]

n. 표현 수단, 배출구
▶ a means of expressing some feelings

2. update [ʌpdéit]

v. 새롭게 하다
n. 새롭게 함, 갱신
▶ to improve something by adding new material

3. download [dáunlòud]

v. 다운로드하다
▶ to take something from the Internet and keep it on one's computer

4. component [kəmpóunənt]

n. 구성요소 a. 구성하는
▶ one piece of an object made of several pieces

5. classical [klǽsikəl]

a. 고전의, 클래식의
▶ traditional in style
▶ classical music 고전 음악

6. combine [kəmbáin]

v. 결합하다
▶ to put two or more things together
▶ combination n. 결합

7. phenomenal [finάmənəl]

a. 놀랄 만한
▶ extremely good, amazing
▶ phenomenon n. 현상

▶ 외우면서 단어를 2번씩 써보세요!

8 **blog** [blá:g]
n. 블로그
▶ a personal website that one writes about oneself

9 **positive** [pázətiv]
a. 긍정적인
▶ good and pleasant

10 **complimentary** [kàmpləméntəri]
a. 칭찬하는, 무료의
▶ expressing nice things to somebody, expressing admiration for something
▷ compliment n. 칭찬

11 **ingenious** [indʒíːnjəs]
a. 독창적인
▶ extremely clever, creative
▷ ingenuity n. 독창성

12 **delighted** [diláitid]
a. 즐거운
▶ very pleased and happy
▷ light v. 기쁘게 하다 n. 기쁨, 즐거움
▷ delightful a. 유쾌한

13 **gratifying** [grǽtəfàiiŋ]
a. 만족스러운
▶ satisfying, feeling pleasure
▷ gratify v. 만족시키다

14 **warn** [wɔːrn]
v. 경고하다
▶ to tell someone not to do something

15 delete [dilíːt]

v. 삭제하다
- ▶ to remove something from one's computer or website
- ▷ deletion n. 삭제

16 confused [kənfjúːzd]

a. 혼란스러운
- ▶ unaware of what is happening or what to do
- ▷ confuse v. 혼동하다, 혼란시키다
- ▷ confusion n. 혼란

17 material [mətíəriəl]

n. 자료
- ▷ component, substance

18 cybercop [sáibərkáp]

n. 사이버 경찰
- ▶ a person who monitors the Internet looking for anything illegal

19 defect [difékt]

n. 결함
- ▶ a mistake or an error
- ▷ defective a. 결함이 있는

20 illegal [ilíːgəl]

a. 불법의
- ▶ against the law, unlawful
- ▷ illegally ad. 불법으로

21 copyright [kápiràit]

n. 저작권
- ▶ the right to use or reproduce a piece of writing or music

▶ 외우면서 단어를 2번씩 써보세요!

22 utilize [júːtəlàiz]
v. 사용하다
▶ to make use of something
▶ utilization n. 이용, 활용

23 property [prápərti]
n. 재산
▶ possessions, assets

24 theft [θeft]
n. 절도
▶ the crime of stealing

25 assert [əsə́ːrt]
v. 강력히 주장하다
▶ to say something forcefully, to insist
▶ assertion n. 주장, 확언

26 sue [suː]
v. 고소하다
▶ to start a legal case against someone

27 infringe [infríndʒ]
v. 침해하다, 위반하다
▶ to do something that is against the law
▶ nfringement n. 위반
▶ infringe on ~을 침해하다, 위반하다

28 consent [kənsént]
n. 동의 v. 동의하다
▶ the agreement to do something
▶ consenter n. 동의자, 승낙자

Exercise

A 주어진 뜻에 해당하는 단어를 보기에서 찾아 쓰세요.

> component   download   outlet   blog   warn
> delete   cybercop   copyright   assert   infringe

① one piece of an object made of several pieces ________________
② a means of expressing some feelings ________________
③ to do something that is against the law ________________
④ a person who monitors the Internet looking for anything illegal ________________
⑤ to tell someone not to do something ________________
⑥ the right to use or reproduce a piece of writing or music ________________
⑦ to say something forcefully, to insist ________________
⑧ to remove something from one's computer or website ________________
⑨ to take something from the Internet and keep it on one's computer ________________
⑩ a personal website that one writes about oneself ________________

B 단어의 관계에 맞게 빈칸을 채우세요.

① combine : ________________ = 결합하다 : 결합
② phenomenal : phenomenon = 놀랄 만한 : ________________
③ ingenious : ingenuity= 독창적인 : ________________
④ delighted : delightful = 즐거운 : ________________
⑤ defect : ________________ = 결함 : 결함이 있는
⑥ ________________ : illegally = 불법의 : 불법으로
⑦ utilize : utilization = ________________ : 활용
⑧ consent : ________________ = 동의, 동의하다 : 동의자

C 의미가 같도록 알맞은 단어를 넣어 문장을 완성하세요.

1. For a few weeks, I ________________ my own blog with music and photos.
   몇 주 동안, 나는 내 블로그의 음악과 사진을 업데이트했어.

2. Sometimes I matched ________________ music with the Volcanoes' photos.
   가끔 나는 고전 음악과 그에 어울리는 볼케이노의 사진을 맞추었어.

3. They left quite ________________ and complimentary messages.
   그들은 꽤 긍정적이고 칭찬하는 메시지를 남겼어.

4. It was ________________ to entertain others.
   다른 사람들을 즐겁게 하는 것이 만족스러웠어

5. There was a written message, "You're not allowed to use these ________________ ."
   메시지에는 "당신은 이 자료를 사용할 수 없습니다"라고 쓰여 있었어.

6. Are there any ________________ in my materials?
   제 자료에 뭔가 결함이 있나요?

7. Other people's creations should be treated like personal ________________ .
   다른 사람들의 창작물은 개인적인 재산으로 취급되어야 해.

8. The owner may try to ________________ you for money.
   주인은 돈을 받으려고 너를 고소하려고 할지도 몰라.

D 녹음된 내용을 듣고, 다음 빈칸에 들어갈 단어나 표현을 쓰세요.

Dear Diary,

Blogging is an __________ for my creative ideas. ● For a few weeks, I __________ my own blog with music and photos. ● I __________ music and the Volcanoes' photos. ● Then I paired the two __________, music and photos. ● Sometimes I matched __________ music with the Volcanoes' photos. ● I spent a few hours combining the best pairs. ● The results were __________. ● Every day over 400 people visited my __________. ● They left quite __________ and __________ messages. ● Someone wrote that my materials were __________. ● I was __________ to read the messages. ● It was __________ to entertain others. ● Today I found a __________ message. ● Some music files had been __________. ● I was very __________. ● There was a written message, "You're not allowed to use these __________."

Bomi: What's wrong? ● Am I going to be arrested by __________? ● Are there any __________ in my materials? ● Mom, why do they think my materials are __________?

Mom: It's related to __________ laws.

Bomi: But I didn't __________ the materials for anything other than my personal interest.

Mom: Other people's creations should be treated like personal __________. ● If you used the materials without the owner's permission, it's like __________. ● If someone __________ copyright properties of their materials, you have to give it back to them. ● The owner may try to __________ you for money.

Bomi: I didn't know I was __________ on their copyright. ● From now on, I'll obtain their __________ before I use someone else's materials.

▶ 1단계 : 먼저 그림을 보고, 이 장의 에피소드를 추측해 보세요.

→ **implement cutting-edge technologies** ●

→ **watch news about fake cell phones** ●

2단계 : 녹음 내용을 들으며, 추측한 에피소드와 비교해 보세요. 

Ｄａｄ : We need to renew our passports.

Bomi: You said they only need to be extended.

Ｄａｄ : New passports would be safer. ● It's because to prevent forgery cutting-edge technologies, like holograms, are being implemented.

Dad said this right after the news that forgeries had been found. Korean cell phones are popular. ● In some countries, they almost monopolize the market. ● Today we watched news about fake cell phones. ● Evidently, the logos and designs on these cell phones are identical to Korean cell phones. ● Consumers can be tricked, believing that they are purchasing genuine Korean products. ● How come this happened?

Sadly, some Koreans were also accused of doing this. ● They have allegedly been deeply involved in this matter. ● Allegedly, they conspired with foreign business people. ● They might expect to receive a fortune in return for this. ● But the financial losses of Korean companies are immeasurable. ● If these traitors are found guilty, they should be forced to compensate for the companies' losses. ● I'm worried that the integrity of Korean products is being harmed. ● What if people's view of Korean products is tarnished?

Bomi: Can it lead to diplomatic disputes?

Ｄａｄ : I think so. ● It could even develop into hostility between the involved countries. ● Forgery laws must be enforced.

Bomi: I think the laws should be reinforced. ● I didn't know that fake products could bring about so many problems.

1 renew [rinjúː]

v. 갱신하다

▶ to get a new passport, a license, or other document
▶ renewable a. 갱신할 수 있는

2 extend [iksténd]

v. 연장하다

▶ to make something last longer than before
▶ extension n. 연장
▶ extensive a. 광범위한

3 passport [pǽspòːrt]

n. 여권

▶ a document that lets one travel to other countries

4 cutting-edge [kʌ́tiŋ edʒ]

a. 최첨단의

▶ of the very newest technology, state-of-the-art

5 implement [ímpləmənt]

v. 이행하다

▶ to put into action

6 forgery [fɔ́ːrdʒəri]

n. 위조품, 위조

▶ a fake; the crime of forging money or documents
▶ forge v. 위조하다
▶ forger n. 위조자

7 monopolize [mənápəlàiz]

v. 독점하다

▶ to have a very large share of something
▶ monopoly n. 독점

▶ 외우면서 단어를 2번씩 써보세요!

8 fake [feik]
a. 가짜의, 모조의
n. 가짜, 모조품
▶ not real, opposite of genuine

9 evidently [évidəntli]
ad. 분명히, 명백히
▶ apparently
▶ evidence n. 증거
▶ evident a. 명백한

10 trick [trik]
v. 속이다   n. 속임수, 기교
▶ to deceive someone
▶ trickery n. 속임수

11 genuine [dʒénjuin]
a. 진짜의
▶ not fake, real, authentic
▶ genuinely ad. 진정으로

12 accuse [əkjúːz]
v. 고소하다
▶ to charge someone with wrongdoing and put on trial
▶ accusation n. 고소
▶ accuse A of B A를 B로 고소하다

13 allegedly [əlédʒdli]
ad. 주장에 의하면
▶ based on someone's assumption
▶ allege v. 주장하다
▶ allegation n. 주장
▶ alleged a. 주장된

▶ 3단계 : 외우면서 단어를 2번씩 써보세요!

⑭ conspire [kənspáiər]

v. 공모하다, 음모를 꾸미다

▶ to make a secret agreement to do something bad
▶ conspiracy n. 음모
▶ conspirator n. 음모자

_______________   _______________

⑮ in return for [in ritə́ːrn fɔːr]

～에 대한 대가로

▶ as a compensation for

_______________   _______________

⑯ immeasurable [iméʒərəbəl]

a. 헤아릴 수 없는

▶ unable to measure or calculate

_______________   _______________

⑰ traitor [tréitər]

n. 반역자

▶ a person who betrays their country or friends

_______________   _______________

⑱ compensate [kámpənsèit]

v. 보상하다

▶ to make up for a loss
▶ compensation n. 보상

_______________   _______________

⑲ integrity [intégrəti]

n. 완전함, 흠 없음

▶ completeness, absoluteness

_______________   _______________

⑳ tarnish [táːrniʃ]

v. 더럽히다 n. 퇴색, 흠

▶ to damage a reputation
▶ tarnished a. 더럽혀진

_______________   _______________

21 diplomatic [dìpləmǽtik]

a. 외교의

- ▶ relating to different countries
- ▶ diplomacy n. 외교
- ▶ diplomat n. 외교관

____________________ ____________________

22 dispute [dispjúːt]

n. 논쟁 v. 논쟁하다

- ▶ a disagreement between people or countries

____________________ ____________________

23 hostility [hástíləti]

n. 적개심, 적대 행위

- ▶ feeling of disaffection; aggressive behavior
- ▶ hostile a. 적의가 있는, 적개심에 불타는

____________________ ____________________

24 enforce [enfɔ́ːrs]

v. 시행하다

- ▶ to make people obey a law
- ▶ enforcement n. 시행

____________________ ____________________

25 reinforce [rìːinfɔ́ːrs]

v. 강화하다

- ▶ to make something stronger
- ▶ reinforcement n. 보강, 강화

____________________ ____________________

A 주어진 뜻에 해당하는 단어를 보기에서 찾아 쓰세요.

> renew   monopolize   trick   accuse   cutting-edge
> traitor   compensate   dispute   enforce   immeasurable

① to charge someone with wrongdoing and put on trial   _____________
② to make up for a loss   _____________
③ of the very newest technology, state-of-the-art   _____________
④ to have a very large share of something   _____________
⑤ unable to measure or calculate   _____________
⑥ a person who betrays their country or friends   _____________
⑦ a disagreement between people or countries   _____________
⑧ to get a new passport, a license, or other document   _____________
⑨ to make people obey a law   _____________
⑩ to deceive someone   _____________

B 단어의 관계에 맞게 빈칸을 채우세요.

① extend : extensive = 연장하다 : _____________
② forgery : _____________ = 위조품 : 위조자
③ evidently : _____________ = 분명히 : 증거
④ allegedly : allege = 주장에 의하면 : _____________
⑤ conspire : conspiracy = _____________ : 음모
⑥ compensate : _____________ = 보상하다 : 보상
⑦ diplomatic : _____________ = 외교의 : 외교관
⑧ _____________ : hostile = 적개심 : 적의가 있는

C 의미가 같도록 알맞은 단어를 넣어 문장을 완성하세요.

1. New _____________ would be safer.
   새 여권이 더 안전할 거야.

2. It's because to prevent forgery cutting-edge technologies, like holograms, are being ___________.
   위조를 방지하려고 홀로그램 같은 최첨단 기술이 사용되기 때문이야.

3. Today we watched news about _____________ cell phones.
   오늘 우리는 가짜 휴대 전화에 관한 뉴스를 보았다.

4. Consumers can be tricked, believing that they are purchasing __________ Korean products.
   소비자들은 속아서 자신들이 진짜 한국 제품을 구입한다고 믿을 수도 있다.

5. They might expect to receive a fortune _____________ this.
   그들은 이것에 대한 대가로 큰 돈을 받기를 기대했을 것이다.

6. I'm worried that the _____________ of Korean products is being harmed.
   나는 한국 제품의 완전함에 흠이 갈까 걱정이다.

7. What if people's view of Korean products is _____________?
   만일 한국 제품에 대한 사람들의 생각이 안 좋아지면 어떻게 하지?

8. I think the laws should be _____________.
   그 법은 강화되어야겠어요.

D 녹음된 내용을 듣고, 다음 빈칸에 들어갈 단어나 표현을 쓰세요.

Ｄａｄ: We need to ____________ our passports.

Bomi: You said they only need to be ____________.

Ｄａｄ: New ________________ would be safer. ● It's because to prevent forgery ________________ technologies, like holograms, are being ______________.

Dad said this right after the news that _________ had been found. Korean cell phones are popular. ● In some countries, they almost _________ the market. ● Today we watched news about _________ cell phones. ● _________, the logos and designs on these cell phones are identical to Korean cell phones. ● Consumers can be ________, believing that they are purchasing _________ Korean products. ● How come this happened?

Sadly, some Koreans were also ____________ of doing this. ● They have __________ been deeply involved in this matter. ● Allegedly, they ____________ with foreign business people. ● They might expect to receive a fortune _________ this. ● But the financial losses of Korean companies are _______________. ● If these ________ are found guilty, they should be forced to ____________ for the companies' losses. ● I'm worried that the ____________ of Korean products is being harmed. ● What if people's view of Korean products is ____________?

Bomi: Can it lead to _________ ____________?

Ｄａｄ: I think so. ● It could even develop into _________ between the involved countries. ● Forgery laws must be _________.

Bomi: I think the laws should be _________. ● I didn't know that fake products could bring about so many problems.

■ 녹음을 듣고, 해당하는 단어와 뜻을 쓰세요.

1	단어:	뜻:	2	단어:	뜻:
3	단어:	뜻:	4	단어:	뜻:
5	단어:	뜻:	6	단어:	뜻:
7	단어:	뜻:	8	단어:	뜻:
9	단어:	뜻:	10	단어:	뜻:
11	단어:	뜻:	12	단어:	뜻:
13	단어:	뜻:	14	단어:	뜻:
15	단어:	뜻:	16	단어:	뜻:
17	단어:	뜻:	18	단어:	뜻:
19	단어:	뜻:	20	단어:	뜻:
21	단어:	뜻:	22	단어:	뜻:
23	단어:	뜻:	24	단어:	뜻:
25	단어:	뜻:	26	단어:	뜻:
27	단어:	뜻:	28	단어:	뜻:
29	단어:	뜻:	30	단어:	뜻:

Voca Plus

접두사 over- / dis-

over-는 '무언가를 지나치게 하다'라는 뜻의 단어를 만드는 접두사이다.
dis-는 'apart,' 'not'이라는 뜻의 접두사로, '무언가를 제거하다'라는 뜻의 단어 혹은 반의어를 만든다.

over-

eat 먹다
over + eat = overeat 과식하다
ex) I always end up overeating during the holidays.
나는 늘 연휴 동안 결국은 과식하게 된다.

- **work** 일하다 — **overwork** 과도하게 일을 시키다
- **burden** 부담시키다 — **overburden** 지나치게 부담시키다
- **sleep** 잠을 자다 — **oversleep** 늦잠 자다
- **flow** 흐르다 — **overflow** 넘쳐 흐르다
- **step** 한 걸음 내디디다 — **overstep** 지나치게 가다, 한도를 넘다
- **estimate** 평가하다 — **overestimate** 과대 평가하다
- **dose** 복용량 — **overdose** 과대 복용

dis-

agree 일치하다
dis + agree = disagree 일치하지 않다
ex) The first witness' testimony disagreed with the second witness'.
첫 번째 증인의 증언은 두 번째 증인의 증언과 일치하지 않았다.

- **close** 닫다 — **disclose** 드러내다, 폭로하다
- **arm** 무장시키다 — **disarm** 무장을 해제하다
- **allow** 허락하다 — **disallow** 금하다
- **approve** 찬성하다 — **disapprove** 찬성하지 않다
- **lodge** 묵게 하다 — **dislodge** 이동시키다, 제거하다
- **infect** 감염시키다 — **disinfect** 소독하다
- **grace** 기품, 고상함 — **disgrace** 불명예, 망신

On a Passport 여권에서

+ **surname** 성

+ **given name** 이름

+ **nationality** 국적

+ **date of birth** 생년월일

+ **sex** 성

+ **date of issue** 발행일

+ **date of expiry** 만기일

Unit 19. Hoony wants to explore outer space.

Nature and Space

▶ 1단계 : 먼저 그림을 보고, 이 장의 에피소드를 추측해 보세요.

→ **observe a lunar eclipse**

think aliens will abduct kids ←

→ **investigate the whole galaxy**

Dear Diary,

Yesterday my family observed an amazing event. ● It was a total lunar eclipse. ● The earth, sun and moon were all aligned. ● This kind of celestial event doesn't happen very often. ● While observing, Hoony said that he wanted to explore other planets in outer space. ● He thought it would be fun to communicate with aliens. ● Seri asked Hoony, "Do you remember we thought aliens would abduct kids?" ● Hoony and Seri made their own game titled Extra-Terrestrials. ● They named their team Expedition from Mars. ● They pretended to be Martians.

In the game, they were aliens exploring the solar system. ● They used Hoony's rocket and called it an artificial satellite. ● In their game, the artificial satellite was orbiting the solar system. ● They called several balls meteorites. ● They made the earth collide with the meteorites by throwing balls at one another. ● They called this event doomsday. ● If doomsday happened, all the people on earth would be in jeopardy. ● It would be catastrophic.

Later we read a book about astronomy. ● In the book, astronomically significant events were described in chronological order. ● It told us about events that had happened over the last few decades. ● Among them, the explosion of the spacecraft in 1986 was the most shocking. ● It was funny to read about the animals that were launched into space. ● We talked about what happened to the animals in space, where there is little gravity. ● We looked at pictures of the animals whose heads sometimes became swollen. ● According to the book, it was because their blood became concentrated in their heads in space. ● We wondered if it was possible to explore the whole galaxy. ● Hoony thought we could investigate the whole galaxy by sending space probes. ● Hoony, you are omitting one important fact. ● Our universe is vast.

▶ 3단계 : 외우면서 단어를 2번씩 써보세요!

1 eclipse [iklíps]

n. (해 · 달의) 식

▶ an event where the earth comes between the sun and the moon so that you cannot see the moon
▶ a lunar eclipse 월식
▶ a solar eclipse 일식

2 align [əláin]

v. 정렬시키다

▶ to position objects into one straight line
▶ alignment n. 정렬

3 celestial [siléstʃəl]

a. 하늘의, 천체의

▶ relating to the sky and stars

4 explore [iksplɔ́:r]

v. 탐험하다

▶ to investigate an area to find something
▶ exploration n. 탐험
▶ explorer n. 탐험가

5 outer space [áutər speis]

외계

▶ the area outside the earth's atmosphere

6 alien [éiljən]

n. 외계인 a. 외국의

▶ a creature from outer space

7 abduct [æbdʌ́kt]

v. 유괴하다

▶ to kidnap
▶ abduction n. 유괴

▶ 외우면서 단어를 2번씩 써보세요!

8 Extra-Terrestrial
[ékstrə təréstriəl]

n. 외계인 a. 지구 밖의
▶ a creature that exists in another part of the universe

_____________ _____________

9 expedition [èkspədíʃən]
n. 탐험대, 원정대
▶ people on a journey

_____________ _____________

10 Martian [mɑ́ːrʃən]
n. 화성인
▶ an alien who lives on the planet Mars

_____________ _____________

11 solar system [sóulər sístəm]
태양계
▶ the earth and all the planets that move around the sun

_____________ _____________

12 artificial satellite
[ɑ̀ːrtəfíʃəl sǽtəlàit]
인공위성
▶ an object sent into space to send information

_____________ _____________

13 orbit [ɔ́ːrbit]
v. 궤도를 그리며 돌다
n. 궤도
▶ to move in a circle around another object

_____________ _____________

14 meteorite [míːtiəràit]
n. 운석
▶ a large rock that floats in space

_____________ _____________

15 collide [kəláid]

v. 충돌하다

▶ to crash into something
▷ collision n. 충돌

_______________ _______________

16 doomsday [dú:mzdèi]

n. 최후의 심판일

▶ a day when a terrible and harmful event will happen

_______________ _______________

17 jeopardy [dʒépərdi]

n. 위험

▶ danger, trouble
▷ jeopardize v. 위험에 빠뜨리다
▷ in jeopardy 위험에 처한, 위급한

_______________ _______________

18 catastrophic [kæ̀təstráfik]

a. 큰 재앙의

▶ very dangerous, extremely harmful
▷ catastrophe n. 큰 재앙

_______________ _______________

19 astronomy [əstránəmi]

n. 천문학

▶ the scientific study of the stars and planets
▷ astronomical a. 천문학적인
▷ astronomically ad. 천문학적으로

_______________ _______________

20 chronological [krànəládʒikəl]

a. 연대순의

▶ arranged according to the sequence of events occurred
▷ chronology n. 연대기

_______________ _______________

21 decade [dékeid]

n. 10년

▶ a period of ten years

_______________ _______________

▶ 외우면서 단어를 2번씩 써보세요!

22 explosion [iksplóuʒən]

n. 폭발

▶ an eruption, a blast
▷ explode v. 폭발하다
▷ explosive a. 폭발성이 있는

23 launch [lɔːntʃ]

v. 쏘아 올리다, 발사하다

▶ to send something into the air or into space

24 gravity [grǽvəti]

n. 중력

▶ the force that makes things fall to the ground
▷ gravitation n. 중력
▷ gravitational a. 중력의

25 swell [swel]

v. 부풀다, 팽창하다

▶ to become larger
▷ swelling n. 팽창

26 galaxy [gǽləksi]

n. 은하계

▶ a group of stars in the universe
▷ galactic a. 은하계의

27 space probe [speis proub]

우주 탐사선

▶ a small rocket sent into space to investigate

28 omit [oumít]

v. 빠뜨리다, 생략하다

▶ to leave something out
▷ omission n. 생략

Exercise

A 주어진 뜻에 해당하는 단어를 보기에서 찾아 쓰세요.

> outer space   alien   Extra-Terrestrials   solar system   orbit
> doomsday   chronological   launch   space probe   gravity

① the earth and all the planets that move around the sun   __________
② arranged according to the sequence of events occurred   __________
③ the area outside the earth's atmosphere   __________
④ the force that makes things fall to the ground   __________
⑤ to move in a circle around another object   __________
⑥ to send something into the air or into space   __________
⑦ a creature that exists in another part of the universe   __________
⑧ a small rocket sent into space to investigate   __________
⑨ a day when a terrible and harmful event will happen   __________
⑩ a creature from outer space   __________

B 단어의 관계에 맞게 빈칸을 채우세요.

① explore : __________ = 탐험하다 : 탐험
② abduct : abduction = __________ : 유괴
③ align : __________ = 정렬시키다 : 정렬
④ collide : __________ = 충돌하다 : 충돌
⑤ catastrophic : catastrophe = 큰 재앙의 : __________
⑥ astronomy : __________ = 천문학 : 천문학적으로
⑦ __________ : explode = 폭발 : 폭발하다
⑧ galaxy : galactic = 은하계 : __________

C 의미가 같도록 알맞은 단어를 넣어 문장을 완성하세요.

1. It was a total lunar __________ .
   전체 월식이었다.

2. This kind of __________ event doesn't happen very often.
   하늘에서 일어나는 이런 종류의 현상은 자주 일어나지 않는다.

3. They named their team __________ from Mars.
   그들은 그들의 팀을 화성에서 온 탐험대라고 이름붙였다.

4. They used Hoony's rocket and called it an __________ .
   그들은 후니의 로케트를 사용했고 그것을 인공위성이라고 불렀다.

5. They called several balls __________ .
   그들은 여러 개의 공을 운석이라고 불렀다.

6. If doomsday happened, all the people on earth would be in __________ .
   만일 최후의 심판일이 온다면, 지구에 사는 모든 사람들은 위험에 처하겠지.

7. We looked at pictures of the animals whose heads sometimes became __________ .
   우리는 동물들의 그림을 보았는데 머리가 가끔 부풀어 올라 있었다.

8. Hoony, you are __________ one important fact.
   후니, 너는 중요한 사실 하나를 빠뜨렸어.

Date	Score

D 녹음된 내용을 듣고, 다음 빈칸에 들어갈 단어나 표현을 쓰세요.

Dear Diary,

Yesterday my family observed an amazing event. ● It was a total ___________ ___________. ● The earth, sun and moon were all ___________. ● This kind of ___________ event doesn't happen very often. ● While observing, Hoony said that he wanted to ___________ other ___________ in outer space. ● He thought it would be fun to communicate with ___________. ● Seri asked Hoony, "Do you remember we thought aliens would ___________ kids?" ● Hoony and Seri made their own game titled ___________. ● They named their team ___________ from Mars. ● They pretended to be ___________.

In the game, they were aliens exploring the ___________. ● They used Hoony's rocket and called it an ___________. ● In their game, the artificial satellite was ___________ the solar system. ● They called several balls ___________. ● They made the earth ___________ with the meteorites by throwing balls at one another. ● They called this event ___________. ● If doomsday happened, all the people on earth would be ___________. ● It would be ___________.

Later we read a book about ___________. ● In the book, astronomically significant events were described in ___________ order. ● It told us about events that had happened over the last few ___________. ● Among them, the ___________ of the spacecraft in 1986 was the most shocking. ● It was funny to read about the animals that were ___________ into space. ● We talked about what happened to the animals in space, where there is little ___________. ● We looked at pictures of the animals whose heads sometimes became ___________. ● According to the book, it was because their blood became concentrated In their heads in space. ● We wondered if it was possible to explore the whole ___________. ● Hoony thought we could investigate the whole galaxy by sending ___________ ___________. ● Hoony, you are ___________ one important fact. ● Our universe is vast.

Nature and Space

▶ 1단계 : 먼저 그림을 보고, 이 장의 에피소드를 추측해 보세요.

→ **hold a special ceremony**

→ **take care of environment**

Episode

Dear Diary,

Sometimes we tend to take nature for granted, not realizing how valuable it is. ● We often misuse nature, calculating only its economic value. ● Our school held a special ceremony on Arbor Day. ● All the students were wearing masks because of the yellow dust. ● Our school principal inaugurated the event by planting a tree. ● After the tree planting, he talked about the effects pollutants from yellow dust have on us. ● He explained why yellow dust had increased in our peninsula. ● He asked us what caused the erosion of soil. ● He also asked us what caused landslides and floods. ● We answered unanimously, "deforestation." ● He emphasized again that we should be vigilant in taking care of our environment. ● He also added, "If we don't preserve nature, it will counterattack humans." ● After the ceremony, our class went to a theme park. ● It was a popular eco-friendly park. ● There were many species of plants and animals. ● Animals, such as rabbits, were living in colonies. ● Our teacher said that this area used to be a landfill. ● Where did the garbage go? ● It seemed unaccountable. ● How on earth did plants grow in the contaminated soil? ● The soil must surely have been toxic. ● Actually, huge efforts had been made to successfully neutralize the toxins in the soil. ● Thanks to the neutralization efforts, the barren land had become a park. ● The landscape had completely changed. ● Some endangered species are now able to live there. ● That means their habitats have recovered. ● In this place, they will not become extinct. ● It made me very happy to see the theme park's conservation efforts.

1 **take for granted**
[téik fɔːr grǽntìd]
당연한 일로 생각하다
▶ to accept something as normal without thinking about it

2 **calculate** [kǽlkjəlèit]
v. 계산하다, 평가하다
▶ to decide how much money something is worth
▷ calculation n. 계산

3 **Arbor Day** [áːrbər déiæk]
식목일
▶ a special day when many people publicly plant trees

4 **yellow dust** [jélou dʌst]
황사
▶ yellow colored dirt that the wind blows to Korea from China

5 **inaugurate** [inɔ́ːgjərèit]
v. ~식을 행하다
▶ to start an event with a special ceremony
▷ inauguration n. 개회
▷ inaugural a. 개회의

6 **pollutant** [pəlúːtənt]
n. 오염물질
▶ poisonous or harmful chemical which can make one sick
▷ pollute v. 오염시키다
▷ pollution n. 오염

7 **peninsula** [pinínʃələ]
n. 반도
▶ a long narrow piece of land joined to a main land, surrounded with water

▶ 외우면서 단어를 2번씩 써보세요!

8 erosion [iróuʒən]

n. 침식

▶ wearing away of soil through wind and rain
▶ erode v. 침식하다

____________ ____________

9 landslide [lǽndslàid]

n. 산사태

▶ a large amount of soil and rock that falls down the side of a mountain

____________ ____________

10 flood [flʌd]

n. 홍수
v. 범람하다

▶ a large amount of water that covers an area which is usually dry

____________ ____________

11 deforestation [diːfɔ́ːristéiʃən]

n. 삼림 벌채

▶ removal of all the trees from a piece of land, logging
▶ deforest v. 삼림을 벌채하다

____________ ____________

12 vigilant [vídʒələnt]

a. 주의하는, 방심하지 않는

▶ careful, watchful
▶ vigilance n. 조심

____________ ____________

13 counterattack [káuntərətæ̀k]

v. 역습하다
n. 역습, 반격

▶ to attack someone who has attacked you.

____________ ____________

14 theme park [θiːm pɑːrk]

테마 파크

▶ a large outdoor area where all the activities are usually based on a particular theme

____________ ____________

▶ **3단계 : 외우면서 단어를 2번씩 써보세요!**

15 eco-friendly [éko fréndli]
a. 친환경의
▶ not damaging the environment

16 species [spí:ʃi(:)z]
n. 종, 종류
▶ a type of plant or animal of the same family or category

17 colony [káləni]
n. 집단, 군체
▶ a group of people or animals that live together

18 landfill [lǽndfil]
n. 쓰레기 매립지
▶ a place where garbage is dumped then disposed of

19 unaccountable [Ànəkáuntəbəl]
a. 설명할 수 없는
▶ difficult to believe or explain
▶ account v. 설명하다 n. 설명
▶ accountable a. 설명할 수 있는

20 contaminated [kəntǽmənèitd]
a. 오염된
▶ polluted, poisonous
▶ contaminate v. 오염시키다
▶ contamination n. 오염

21 toxic [táksik]
a. 유독한, 독(성)의
▶ very harmful, poisonous
▶ toxin n. 독소

22 neutralize [njúːtrəlàiz]

v. 중화하다

▶ to reduce acidic levels or effects of something
▶ neutralization n. 중화
▶ neutral a. 중성의

23 barren [bǽrən]

a. 불모의

▶ unprofitable, fruitless, opposite of fertile

24 landscape [lǽndskèip]

n. 경관

▶ all the features that are seen in an area of land

25 endangered species [endéindʒərd spíːʃi(ː)z]

멸종 위기에 있는 동식물

▶ a type of plant or animal that has almost died out
▶ endanger v. 위험에 빠뜨리다
▶ endangered a. 멸종될 위기에 있는

26 habitat [hǽbətæ̀t]

n. 서식지

▶ the natural environment where a certain animal or plant lives

27 extinct [ikstíŋkt]

a. 멸종된

▶ dead and gone
▶ extinction n. 멸종

28 conservation [kànsəːrvéiʃən]

n. 보호, 보존

▶ saving and protecting the environment
▶ conserve v. 보호하다

Exercise

A 주어진 뜻에 해당하는 단어를 보기에서 찾아 쓰세요.

> Arbor Day   inaugurate   peninsula   flood   deforestation
> species   landfill   landscape   habitat   barren

① a large amount of water that covers an area which is usually dry   __________

② a place where garbage is dumped then disposed of   __________

③ to start an event with a special ceremony   __________

④ a type of plant or animal of the same family or category   __________

⑤ all the features that are seen in an area of land   __________

⑥ a long narrow piece of land joined to a main land   __________

⑦ unprofitable, fruitless, opposite of fertile   __________

⑧ removal of all the trees from a piece of land, logging   __________

⑨ the natural environment where a certain animal or plant lives   __________

⑩ a special day when many people publicly plant trees   __________

B 단어의 관계에 맞게 빈칸을 채우세요.

① pollutant : _______________ = 오염물질 : 오염

② calculate : calculation = _______________ : 계산

③ vigilant : vigilance = 주의하는 : _______________

④ erosion : _______________ = 침식 : 침식하다

⑤ _______________ : contamination = 오염된 : 오염

⑥ toxic : toxin = 유독한 : _______________

⑦ neutralize : neutral = 중화하다 : _______________

⑧ _______________ : extinction = 멸종된 : 멸종

C 의미가 같도록 알맞은 단어를 넣어 문장을 완성하세요.

1. Sometimes we tend to ________nature _______, not realizing how valuable it is.
   가끔 우리는 자연이 존재하는 것을 당연하게 생각하고 그것이 얼마나 중요한지 깨닫지 못해.

2. All the students were wearing masks because of the _______________.
   모든 학생들은 황사 때문에 마스크를 쓰고 있었어.

3. He also added, "If we don't preserve nature, it will __________ humans."
   또한 "우리가 자연을 보존하지 않으면, 그것이 인간을 역습할 것입니다"라고 덧붙이셨어.

4. He also asked us what caused _______________ and floods.
   그는 또한 산사태와 홍수의 원인을 묻기도 하셨어.

5. It was a popular _______________ park.
   그곳은 인기 있는 친환경 공원이었어.

6. Where did the garbage go? It seemed _______________.
   쓰레기는 어디로 갔지? 그것은 설명이 안될 것 같았어.

7. Some _______________ are now able to live there.
   몇몇 멸종 위기의 동식물들은 지금은 그곳에서 살 수 있어.

8. Animals, such as rabbits, were living in _______________.
   토끼와 같은 동물들은 집단으로 서식하고 있었어.

	Date	Score

D 녹음된 내용을 듣고, 다음 빈칸에 들어갈 단어나 표현을 쓰세요.

Dear Diary,

Sometimes we tend to __________ nature __________ __________, not realizing how valuable it is. ● We often misuse nature, __________ only its economic value. ● Our school held a special ceremony on __________ __________. ● All the students were wearing masks because of the __________ __________. ● Our school principal inaugurated the event by planting a tree. ● After the tree planting, he talked about the effects __________ __________ from yellow dust have on us. ● He explained why yellow dust had increased in our __________. ● He asked us what caused the __________ of soil. ● He also asked us what caused __________ and __________. ● We answered unanimously, "__________." ● He emphasized again that we should be __________ in taking care of our environment. ● He also added, "If we don't preserve nature, it will __________ humans." ● After the ceremony, our class went to a __________. ● It was a popular __________ park. ● There were many __________ of plants and animals. ● Animals, such as rabbits, were living in __________. ● Our teacher said that this area used to be a __________. ● Where did the garbage go? ● It seemed __________. ● How on earth did plants grow in the __________ soil? ● The soil must surely have been __________. ● Actually, huge efforts had been made to successfully __________ the toxins in the soil. ● Thanks to the neutralization efforts, the __________ land had become a park. ● The __________ had completely changed. ● Some __________ __________ are now able to live there. ● That means their __________ have recovered. ● In this place, they will not become __________. ● It made me very happy to see the theme park's __________ efforts.

Chapter 6

Nature and Space

Unit 21. We can make the earth a better place.

▶ 1단계 : 먼저 그림을 보고, 이 장의 에피소드를 추측해 보세요.

→ **emerge as an alternative**

watch a program featuring a goat ←

→ **have a green thumb**

Dear Diary,

Are economic development and nature incompatible? ● News reports say that we have to reduce the amount of CO_2 emissions. ● Many countries admit that nature preservation is preferable to economic development. ● Large sedan cars powered by gasoline used to be popular. ● Now small-sized hybrid cars are emerging as an alternative to them. ● Companies will have to look for bio-fuels instead of fossil fuels. ● They may feel oppressed. ● But people arelearning the lesson of moderation.

Recently, Seri and I talked about the food crises in some countries. ● Seri used to be a supporter of genetically modified food, believing it could be an answer. ● But frequent exposure to television environment channels changed her view. ● One time she watched a program featuring goats at a cotton plantation. ● The goats were fed genetically modified cotton. ● After prolonged consumption of cotton, some goats were born with deformed legs. ● After watching the program, she now firmly believes that genetically modified food is harmful. ● Since she is health-conscious, she tries not to eat food from genetically modified products.

Seri has a miniature garden of cherry tomatoes. ● She doesn't have a green thumb. ● What is her motive for making her own garden? ● She was just trying to find a way to use our family's leftover food. ● She decided not to discard leftover food. ● Instead, she decided to grow a garden and use it as fertilizer. ● She learned that decomposed food makes the soil richer. ● Her garden is a miniature eco-system. ● As an environmentalist, she often says to me, "No more disposables." ● Thanks to her, I try to refrain from using paper cups and plastic bags.

1 incompatible
[ìnkəmpǽtəbl]
a. 양립할 수 없는, 함께할 수 없는
▶ disagreeing, very different
▶ incompatibility n. 양립할 수 없음, 상반

2 reduce [ridjúːs]
v. 줄이다
▶ to make something smaller in size or amount
▶ reduction n. 경감

3 preservation [prèzərvéiʃn]
n. 보호
▶ protection of something from damage
▶ preserve v. 보호하다

4 power [páuər]
v. 동력을 공급하다
▶ to fuel or provide energy

5 hybrid car
[háibrid kɑːr]
하이브리드 자동차
▶ a car that can use both gasoline and another type of fuel

6 emerge [imə́ːrdʒ]
v. 나타나다
▶ to come out, to appear
▶ emergence n. 출현, 발생
▶ emergency n. 비상사태

7 bio-fuel [báiou fjúːəl]
n. 바이오 연료
▶ the fuel made from newly harvested plants instead of gasoline

⑧ fossil fuel [fásl fjúːəl]

화석 연료

▶ the fuel formed from the decayed remains of plants or animals such as oil and coal

___________________ ___________________

⑨ oppress [əprés]

v. 압박하다

▶ to limit people from doing certain things
▶ oppression n. 압박
▶ oppressive a. 압박하는

___________________ ___________________

⑩ moderation [màdəréiʃən]

n. 절제, 완화

▶ control of one's behavior to prevent excessiveness
▶ moderate a. 알맞은
▶ moderately ad. 온건하게

___________________ ___________________

⑪ crisis [kráisis]

n. 위기

▶ a situation that will cause a lot of harm to people
▶ crises (crisis의 복수형)

___________________ ___________________

⑫ genetically modified food
[dʒinétikəli mádəfàiərd fuːd]

유전자 조작 식품

▶ food made by injecting foreign genes into their genetic codes

___________________ ___________________

⑬ exposure [ikspóuʒər]

n. 노출, 드러냄

▶ being affected by something, putting in view
▶ expose v. 노출시키다, 노출하다

___________________ ___________________

⑭ plantation [plæntéiʃən]

n. 재배지

▶ a large piece of farm used to grow plants

___________________ ___________________

▶ **3단계 : 외우면서 단어를 2번씩 써보세요!**

15 **cotton** [kátn]

n. 목화

▶ a plant which produces fibers used to make cotton cloth

_______________ _______________

16 **prolonged** [prəlɔ́:ŋd]

a. 장기의, 연장된

▶ continuing for a long time
▷ prolong v. 연장하다

_______________ _______________

17 **deformed** [difɔ́:rmd]

a. 기형의

▶ having an unusual shape
▷ deform v. 불구로 만들다, 변형시키다

_______________ _______________

18 **firmly** [fə́:rmli]

ad. 굳게, 확고하게

▶ strongly, inflexibly
▷ firm a. 굳은, 확고한

_______________ _______________

19 **health-conscious** [helθ kánʃəs]

a. 건강에 신경쓰는

▶ taking good care of one's health

_______________ _______________

20 **miniature** [míniə]

a. 소형의 n. 축소모형

▶ small; a small version of a larger thing
▷ miniaturize v. 소형화하다

_______________ _______________

21 **have a green thumb** [hǽv ə grí:n θʌ́m]

원예를 잘하다

▶ be good at gardening

_______________ _______________

22 **motive** [móutiv]

n. 동기

▶ a purpose for doing something
▷ motivate v. 동기를 부여하다
▷ motivation n. 동기 부여

_______________ _______________

▶ 외우면서 단어를 2번씩 써보세요!

23 leftover [léftòuvər]
n. 나머지
▶ some food that remains after people have finished using it

_________________ _________________

24 discard [diská:rd]
v. 버리다
▶ to get rid of something

_________________ _________________

25 fertilizer [fə́:rtəlàizər]
n. 비료
▶ the substance that one puts on soil to make new plants grow better
▶ fertilize v. 비옥하게 하다, 비료를 주다

_________________ _________________

26 decomposed [dì:kəmpóuzd]
a. 분해된
▶ chemically changed and rotten
▶ decompose v. 분해하다
▶ decomposition n. 분해

_________________ _________________

27 eco-system [èkou sístəm]
n. 생태계
▶ ecological community

_________________ _________________

28 disposable [dispóuzəbəl]
n. 일회용 물품
a. 일회용의
▶ the thing that is designed to be thrown away after use
▶ dispose v. 처분하다
▶ disposal n. 처분

_________________ _________________

29 refrain [rifréin]
v. 절제하다, 삼가다
▶ to keep from doing
▶ refrain from ~을 절제하다

_________________ _________________

Exercise

A 주어진 뜻에 해당하는 단어를 보기에서 찾아 쓰세요.

> preservation   hybrid car   moderation   crisis   genetically modified food
> deformed   firmly   leftover   disposable   health-conscious

① food made by injecting foreign genes into their genetic codes   __________
② control of one's behavior to prevent excessiveness   __________
③ some food that remains after people have finished using it   __________
④ a car that can use both gasoline and another type of fuel   __________
⑤ having an unusual shape   __________
⑥ taking good care of one's health   __________
⑦ protection of something from damage   __________
⑧ strongly, inflexibly   __________
⑨ the thing that is designed to be thrown away after use   __________
⑩ a situation that will cause a lot of harm to people   __________

B 단어의 관계에 맞게 빈칸을 채우세요.

① reduce : __________ = 줄이다 : 경감
② emerge : emergency = 나타나다 : __________
③ oppress : oppressive = 압박하다 : __________
④ exposure : expose = __________ : 노출하다
⑤ prolonged : prolong = __________ : 연장하다
⑥ __________ : motivation = 동기 : 동기 부여
⑦ fertilizer : __________ = 비료 : 비료를 주다
⑧ decomposed: __________ = 분해된 : 분해

C 의미가 같도록 알맞은 단어를 넣어 문장을 완성하세요.

1. Are economic development and nature __________ ?
   경제 발전과 자연은 양립할 수 없는 것일까?

2. Large sedan cars __________ by gasoline used to be popular.
   휘발유를 연료로 하는 대형 세단은 인기가 있었어.

3. Companies will have to look for bio-fuels instead of __________ .
   회사들은 화석 연료 대신 바이오 연료를 찾아야 할 거야.

4. One time she watched a program featuring goats at a cotton __________ .
   그녀는 면 재배지에 있는 염소를 특집으로 한 프로그램을 본 적이 있어.

5. The goats were fed genetically modified __________ .
   염소는 유전적으로 조작된 목화를 먹었어.

6. She doesn't __________ .
   그녀는 식물을 잘 키우지 못해.

7. She decided not to __________ leftover food.
   그녀는 남은 음식을 버리지 않기로 결심했어.

8. Her garden is a miniature __________ .
   그녀의 밭은 작은 생태계야.

D 녹음된 내용을 듣고, 다음 빈칸에 들어갈 단어나 표현을 쓰세요.

Dear Diary,

Are economic development and nature ____________? ● News reports say that we have to __________ the amount of CO_2 emissions. ● Many countries admit that nature ______________ is preferable to economic development. ● Large sedan cars ____________ by gasoline used to be popular. ● Now small-sized ________ __________ are emerging as an alternative to them. ● Companies will have to look for ____________ instead of __________ __________. ● They may feel ____________. ● But people are learning the lesson of _____________.

Recently, Seri and I talked about the food __________ in some countries. ● Seri used to be a supporter of _________ _________ _____________, believing it could be an answer. ● But frequent ____________ to television environment channels changed her view. ● One time she watched a program featuring goats at a cotton _____________. ● The goats were fed genetically modified ____________. ● After ____________ consumption of cotton, some goats were born with ____________ legs. ● After watching the program, she now ____________ believes that genetically modified food is harmful. ● Since she is _________________, she tries not to eat food from genetically modified products.

Seri has a __________ garden of cherry tomatoes. ● She doesn't _________ _________ _________ _______. ● What is her ____________ for making her own garden? ● She was just trying to find a way to use our family's ____________ food. ● She decided not to _________ leftover food. ● Instead, she decided to grow a garden and use it as __________. ● She learned that ____________ food makes the soil richer. ● Her garden is a miniature ____________. ● As an environmentalist, she often says to me, "No more ____________." ● Thanks to her, I try to __________ from using paper cups and plastic bags.

Nature and Space

▶ 1단계 : 먼저 그림을 보고, 이 장의 에피소드를 추측해 보세요.

→ **devastate homes and villages**

→ **try to prevent the outbreak of a plague**

Sara emailed me.

Dear Bomi,

An El Niño event caused a super hurricane to hit villages along the Southern coast. ● Residents were told to evacuate the area. ● Nevertheless, a few people insisted on staying home, risking their lives. ● Immense sea waves and huge torrents swept the whole village. ● Most of the villagers were left homeless. ● Their homes and village were devastated. ● The destructive force was formidable. ● It could be compared to the power of a nuclear bomb. ● Victims are facing the problem of scarcity of food, clothing and shelter. ● The media showed us pictures of their agonized faces. ● The extent of the damage continues to expand. ● The government proclaimed it a disaster area. ● After several days, the hurricane's force dwindled. ● Returning villagers sighed wearily. ● There was little trace of their houses and properties. ● Nationwide donations were collected. ● Food and medicine were distributed by humanitarian organizations. ● Wide scale sterilization efforts were made throughout the whole area. ● The authorities are trying to prevent the outbreak of a plague. ● Residents were recommended to drink only boiled water. ● Now the government will provide social welfare to the villagers. ● They will help the villagers to rebuild their homes as quickly as possible in order to prevent social unrest.

어·휘·연·구

1 evacuate [ivǽkjuèit]

v. 비우다, 대피시키다

▶ to move out of a place to a safer place
▷ evacuation n. 비우기, 피난
▷ evacuee n. 피난자

2 nevertheless [nèvərðəlés]

ad. 그럼에도 불구하고

▶ regardless, still

3 risk [risk]

v. 위태롭게 하다 n. 위험

▶ to do something that might be dangerous
▷ risky a. 위험한, 아슬아슬한

4 immense [iméns]

a. 거대한

▶ extremely large
▷ immensity n. 거대
▷ immensely ad. 거대하게

5 torrent [tɔ́ːrənt]

n. 급류

▶ a large amount of water flowing violently
▷ torrential a. 급류의

6 homeless [hóumlis]

a. 집이 없는

▶ not having a place to live

7 devastate [dévəstèit]

v. 철저하게 파괴하다, 황폐화시키다

▶ to destroy an area totally
▷ devastation n. 초토화, 황폐화
▷ devastating a. 파괴적인

▶ 외우면서 단어를 2번씩 써보세요!

8. formidable [fɔ́ːrmidəbəl]
a. 무시무시한
- ▶ powerful, strong
- ▶ formidably ad. 무시무시하게

9. nuclear bomb [njúːkliər bɑm]
핵폭탄
- ▶ a type of weapon that will explode and destroy things

10. scarcity [skɛ́ərsiti]
n. 부족함
- ▶ shortness of supply
- ▶ scarce a. 드문
- ▶ scarcely ad. 드물게

11. shelter [ʃéltər]
n. 대피소, 피난처
- ▶ a place for homeless people; a place that is made to protect people from bad weather or danger

12. agonized [ǽgənàizd]
a. 괴로워하는
- ▶ extremely upset or hurt
- ▶ agonize v. 몹시 괴롭히다
- ▶ agony n. 고통

13. extent [ikstént]
n. 범위
- ▶ the size or scale of something
- ▶ extensive a. 넓은

14. proclaim [proukléim]
v. 선언하다
- ▶ to make something known to public formally
- ▶ proclamation n. 선언

15 dwindle [dwíndl]

v. 감소하다

▶ to become less, to reduce to low levels
▷ dwindling a. 감소하는

16 wearily [wíərəli]

ad. 피곤하게

▶ in a weary manner
▷ weary v. 지치게 하다 a. 피곤한
▷ weariness n. 피곤함

17 trace [treis]

n. 흔적

▶ a sign that shows something existed there

18 nationwide [néiʃənwàid]

a. 전국적인

▶ involving the whole nation

19 humanitarian [hjuːmænətɛ́əriən]

a. 인도주의적인
n. 인도주의자

▶ helping and taking care of other people
▷ humanitarianism n. 인도주의

▶ 외우면서 단어를 2번씩 써보세요!

20 sterilize [stérəlàiz]

v. 소독하다

▶ to clean something so that there is no dirt and germs
▶ sterilization n. 소독
▶ sterile a. 살균한

21 plague [pleig]

n. 전염병

▶ a disease that can quickly spread and kill many people

22 boiled [bɔild]

a. 끓인

▶ heated to the point where liquid turns to gas
▶ boil v. 끓이다

23 welfare [wélfɛ̀ər]

n. 복지

▶ well-being, the health and prosperity

24 rebuild [ri:bíld]

v. 재건하다, 다시 짓다

▶ to build something again

25 unrest [ʌ̀nrést]

n. 불안, 근심

▶ the uneasy state, disturbance

Exercise

A 주어진 뜻에 해당하는 단어를 보기에서 찾아 쓰세요.

> risk   torrent   nuclear bomb   devastate   proclaim
> trace   humanitarian   plague   unrest   rebuild

① to destroy an area totally   ________________
② to build something again   ________________
③ a type of weapon that will explode and destroy things   ________________
④ to make something known to public formally   ________________
⑤ helping and taking care of other people   ________________
⑥ a large amount of water flowing violently   ________________
⑦ the uneasy state, disturbance   ________________
⑧ a sign that shows something existed there   ________________
⑨ to do something that might be dangerous   ________________
⑩ a disease that can quickly spread and kill many people   ________________

B 단어의 관계에 맞게 빈칸을 채우세요.

① evacuate : evacuee = 대피시키다 : ________________
② immense : ________________ = 거대한 : 거대하게
③ scarcity : scarce = ________________ : 드문
④ agonized : agony = 괴로워하는 : ________________
⑤ wearily : ________________ = 피곤하게 : 피곤
⑥ dwindle : dwindling = 감소하다 : ________________
⑦ sterilize : sterile = 소독하다 : ________________
⑧ ________________ : boil = 끓인 : 끓이다

C 의미가 같도록 알맞은 단어를 넣어 문장을 완성하세요.

1. ____________, a few people insisted on staying home, risking their lives.
   그럼에도 불구하고, 몇몇 사람들은 생명을 걸고 집에 남아 있기를 주장했어.

2. Most of the villagers were left ________________ .
   대부분의 마을 사람들은 집을 잃었어.

3. The destructive force was ________________ .
   파괴의 힘은 무시무시했어.

4. The ________________ of the damage continues to expand.
   피해의 범위는 계속 넓어지고 있어.

5. ________________ donations were collected.
   전국적인 기부 물품들이 모아졌어.

6. Now the government will provide social ________________ to the villagers.
   이제 정부는 마을 사람들에게 사회복지 혜택을 줄 거야.

7. Victims are facing the problem of scarcity of food, clothing and __________ .
   희생자들은 음식, 옷, 대피소가 부족한 문제에 당면하게 되었어.

8. Residents were told to ________________ the area.
   주민들은 그 지역에서 떠나라는 이야기를 들었어.

D 녹음된 내용을 듣고, 다음 빈칸에 들어갈 단어나 표현을 쓰세요.

Sara emailed me.

Dear Bomi,

An El Niño event caused a super hurricane to hit villages along the Southern coast. ● Residents were told to ______________ the area. ● ____________, a few people insisted on staying home, ____________ their lives. ● ____________ sea waves and huge ____________ swept the whole village. ● Most of the villagers were left ____________. ● Their homes and village were ____________. ● The destructive force was ____________. ● It could be compared to the power of a ____________. ● Victims are facing the problem of ____________ of food, clothing and ____________. ● The media showed us pictures of their ____________ faces. ● The ____________ of the damage continues to expand. ● The government ____________ it a disaster area. ● After several days, the hurricane's force ____________. ● Returning villagers sighed ____________. ● There was little ____________ of their houses and properties. ● ____________ donations were collected. ● Food and medicine were distributed by ____________ organizations. ● Wide scale ____________ efforts were made throughout the whole area. ● The authorities are trying to prevent the outbreak of a ____________. ● Residents were recommended to drink only ____________ water. ● Now the government will provide social ____________ to the villagers. ● They will help the villagers to ____________ their homes as quickly as possible in order to prevent social ____________.

Total

/ 30

■ 녹음을 듣고, 해당하는 단어와 뜻을 쓰세요.

1	단어:	뜻:	2	단어:	뜻:
3	단어:	뜻:	4	단어:	뜻:
5	단어:	뜻:	6	단어:	뜻:
7	단어:	뜻:	8	단어:	뜻:
9	단어:	뜻:	10	단어:	뜻:
11	단어:	뜻:	12	단어:	뜻:
13	단어:	뜻:	14	단어:	뜻:
15	단어:	뜻:	16	단어:	뜻:
17	단어:	뜻:	18	단어:	뜻:
19	단어:	뜻:	20	단어:	뜻:
21	단어:	뜻:	22	단어:	뜻:
23	단어:	뜻:	24	단어:	뜻:
25	단어:	뜻:	26	단어:	뜻:
27	단어:	뜻:	28	단어:	뜻:
29	단어:	뜻:	30	단어:	뜻:

Voca Plus

접두사 astro- / counter

astro-는 별이나 우주와 관련된 뜻의 단어를 만드는 접두사이다.
counter-는 'against'라는 뜻의 단어로, '무언가에 반대되다'라는 뜻의 단어를 만든다.

astro-

logia ~에 관한
astro + logy = astrology 점성학, 점성술
ex) She has deep faith in astrology.
그녀는 점성술을 굳게 믿는다.

- navigate 항해   astronavigation 우주 비행
- -nomy 학문   astronomy 천문학
- physics 물리학   astrophysics 천체 물리학
- archaeology 고고학   astroarchaeology 천체 고고학
- compass 나침반   astrocompass 천측 나침반
- space 공간   astrospace 우주 공간
- photography 사진술   astrophotography 천체 사진술

counter-

clockwise 시계방향
counter + clockwise = counterclockwise 반 시계방향
ex) The special clock in the clock tower ran counterclockwise.
시계탑에 있는 특이한 시계는 반 시계방향으로 움직였다.

- attack 공격하다   counterattack 반격하다
- act 행동하다   counteract 거스르다, 방해하다
- part 부분   counterpart 한 짝의 한쪽, 상대방
- balance 균형을 잡다   counterbalance 대등하게 하다
- productive 생산적인   counterproductive 비생산적인, 역효과의
- sign 서명하다   countersign 이어서 서명하다
- change 바꾸다   counterchange 교체하다

Culture Plus

In Space   우주에서

+ **space exploration** 우주 탐사

+ **space probe** 우주 탐사기

+ **space flight** 우주 비행

+ **space lab** 우주 실험실

+ **space shuttle** 우주 왕복선

+ **space station** 우주 정거장

+ **lunar module** 달 착륙선

Answer Keys

VOCA EDG

VOCA EDGE SMART_6

Episode

다이어리에게.
마침내, 볼케이노가 아시아 순회공연을 마치고 돌아왔어. 나는 지난 주에 발매된 그들의 새 앨범을 샀어. 나는 오늘 대형 경기장에서 열리는 그들의 콘서트를 보러 갈 거야. 우리 엄마가 나를 거기까지 태워주기로 하셨어.

엄마: 보미, 현수막 잘 챙겨라. 서둘러야겠다. 길이 막히면 어떻게 하니? 좋은 자리 맡으려면 일찍 가야 해. 다른 사람이 네 시야를 막으면 어떻게 하니? 보미, 이 노래는 친숙하구나.
보미: 실은 그들이 몇몇 한국 가요를 다시 불렀어요.
엄마: 힙합 말고 그들은 어떤 장르의 음악을 하고 있니?
보미: 광범위한 음악을 다루고 있어요.

비틀즈의 팬인 엄마는 비틀즈의 음악이 그녀에게 영감을 주었다고 말해. 엄마는 요즘 음악에는 별로 관심이 없으셔. 힙합 음악에는 뭔가 부정적인 것들이 있다고 생각하셔. 매일 아침 나는 볼케이노의 시디를 플레이어에 넣어. 그리고 최면을 걸려는 나의 시도가 효과를 발휘하기 시작해. 이제 엄마는 그들의 음악을 좀 더 받아들이기 시작하는 것 같아. 전 세계적으로 볼케이노의 열혈팬들이 많다는 것을 알고 계셔. 이제 엄마는 그들이 전 세계에서 명성을 떨치고 있다는 것을 알고 계셔. 심지어 일본에서도 유명하다는 것을 알고 계셔.
나는 늘 우리 엄마에게 나의 영웅인 영웅이 사람들을 자석처럼 끌어당긴다고 말해. 그는 음악에 열정적이야. 그는 늘 "음악이 나를 지탱한다"라고 말해. 정말 전문가다운 소리 아닌가? 만일 엄마가 그가 전자기타 연주하는 모습을 보신다면, 감탄하실 거야. 오늘의 콘서트는 의미있어. 수익금은 백혈병 어린이들을 돕는 데 사용될 거야. 그것은 또한 기아로 고통 받는 아이들을 돕는 데에도 쓰일 거야.

Exercise

A

1. release
2. banner
3. block
4. genre
5. renowned
6. range
7. contemporary
8. negative
9. speechless
10. famine

B

1. magnetic
2. 유명한
3. insertion
4. grandeur
5. congested
6. revival
7. 영감
8. 최면술

C

1. famine
2. meaningful
3. electric
4. specialist
5. sustains
6. passionate
7. fanatics
8. receptive

Episode

사라에게.
무엇이 후니를 그렇게 변하게 했을까? 후니는 과학 잡지를 정기구독하고 있어. 심지어 알버트 아인슈타인의 전기도 읽었어. 후니는 물리학의 근본 원리를 아는 것이 중요하다고 생각해. 오늘 후니는 내게 이상한 공식을 보여주었어. 그것은 아인슈타인의 상대성 이론이었어. 후니는 노벨상을 타는 최초의 한국 물리학자가 되기를 바래. 후니는 아주 애국심이 많아지고 있어. 후니는 또물로켓의 성능을 나아지게 하려고 부단한 노력을 하고 있어. 로켓을 가지고 실험하는 데 아주 많은 시간을 보내. 그리고는 후니는 로켓이 손상되지 않도록 선반에 올려놓아. 매일 아침 왁스로 광택까지 내.

보미: 몸체에 왜 쇳조각을 붙이고 있는 거야?
후니: 내 로켓이 가장 오랜 시간 동안 날도록 만들고 있어. 나는 이것을 특별하게 만들 거야. 결국에는 민수의 로켓을 이길 거야.

사라, 네 남동생은 여전히 회장연설하는 걸 좋아하니? 나는 네 남동생이 다섯 명의 다른 후보들과 경쟁해서 학교회장에 당선되길 바래. 일단 네 남동생이 학생들 앞에서 잘하겠다고 공약하면, 학생들이 그에게 투표를 할 거야. 네 남동생은 회장으로 뽑히는 목표를 달성할 수 있을 거야. 나는 네 남동생이 말재주가 있는 것으로 기억하고 있어. 네 남동생은 미국 대사관 앞에서 자신의 능력을 보여주었잖아. 그 당시에 네 남동생은 전쟁 중지를 주장하고 있었어. 네 남동생은 비폭력을 강조하려고 했어. 네 남동생은 분명히 훌륭한 정치인이 될 거야.

Exercise

A

1. statesman
2. halt
3. advocate
4. embassy
5. pledge
6. candidate
7. surpass
8. extraordinary
9. metal
10. intact

B

1. 주기적인
2. election
3. relativity
4. 광을 낸
5. entire
6. patriot
7. 물리학
8. president

C

1. non-violence
2. advocating
3. subscribing
4. biography
5. fundamental
6. formula
7. strenuous
8. intact

Chapter 1 Unit 3

Chapter 1 Unit 4

Episode

보미: 사라, 세상에서 가장 영향력 있는 사람들은 누구라고 생각해? 그리고 어떤 자질이 그들을 유명하게 만들지? 빌 게이츠는 어떻게 그런 천문학적인 양의 돈을 벌었을까? 그는 일종의 직관력 같은 것이 있어서 비즈니스의 미래를 볼 수 있는 것일까? 아니면 그냥 금전만능주의자일 뿐일까?

사라: 그는 금전만능주의자는 아니라고 생각해. 그는 박애주의자야. 그의 재단은 많은 사람들에게 혜택을 주고 있어.

보미: 정말이니? 그렇다면 그는 자비심이 있는 거네. 그의 재단의 일차적인 목표는 뭐야? 천재들을 지원하는 거야?

사라: 맞아. 전 세계에 있는 미래의 과학자들을 지원하고 있어.

보미: 미래의 빌 게이츠를 길러내는구나.

사라: 그래. 그는 사회를 돕겠다고 공약했어.

보미: 네가 관심을 가지고 있는 역사적인 인물들이 있니?

사라: 나는 콜럼버스 같은 탐험가를 만나고 싶어. 그가 왜 미지의 세계를 향해 모험을 나섰는지 물어보고 싶어. 그가 어떻게 그렇게 대단한 역사적인 항해를 해냈는지 궁금해.

보미: 나는 후추 같은 향신료가 그렇게 귀했는지 묻고 싶어. 그리고 "후추 한 상자 가져오면, 제 부하가 되어주겠어요?"라고 물어보고 싶어.

사라: 재밌네. 만일 네가 중국의 진시황제를 만난다면, 뭐라고 할래?

보미: 영원히 살고 싶어 했던 그 황제? "이보게, 독한 액체 좀 그만 마시지 그래? "아니면" 그렇게 잔인하게 군대를 훈련시키는 것 좀 그만두는 게 어때?"라고 말할 거야.

사라: 그렇게 말하면, 너는 추방당할 거야.

보미: 그는 자기가 폭군인 걸 알아야 해. 백성들이 그의 정권 하에 고통받고 있었잖아.

사라: 맞아. 그가 일찍 죽지 않았다면, 자기 나라에서 도망쳐야 했을 수도 있어.

보미: 맞아. 그는 암살당할 수도 있었을 거야.

Exercise

A

1. quality
2. money-oriented
3. foundation
4. throughout
5. nurture
6. commitment
7. figure
8. venture
9. priceless
10. subordinate

B

1. tyranny
2. 독소
3. eternal
4. 황제
5. 항해가
6. merciful
7. 일차적인
8. prodigy

C

1. assassinated
2. fled
3. regime
4. exiled
5. disciplining
6. subordinate
7. prlceless
8. influential

Episode

다이어리에게.

이상적인 배우자를 찾는 게 가능할까? 우리 엄마와 아빠는 비슷한 구석이 전혀 없어: 사실, 두 분의 행동은 여러 가지 면에서 대조가 돼. 아빠는 상당히 시간을 잘 지키셔. 아빠는 약속에 늦으시는 법이 거의 없어. 그렇지만 엄마는 아빠를 만나러 가실 때 항상 늦으셔. 아빠는 엄마가 아는 사람들과 커피를 마시며 꾸물거리기 때문이라고 생각하셔. 내가 아빠라면, 나는 복수를 하기 위해서 일부러 늦게 갈 거야. 보통 아빠는 운전할 때를 제외하고는 엄마보다 더 조심스러워. 지출에 관해 조심스럽게 챙기는 사람은 아빠야. 종종 휴대전화 연체 요금을 내야 하는 사람은 엄마야. 엄마는 요금 납부 기한이 연장되어야 한다고 불평하셔. 그래서 엄마와 아빠는 이런 문제에 대해서 말다툼하셔.

오늘 아침에 아빠는 엄마를 위해서 자동 이체 서비스를 신청할 거라고 말씀하셨어. 엄마는 이상적인 커플은 친밀한 유대감이 있어야 한다고 말씀하셨어. 나는 왜 많은 커플들이 비슷한 점보다 다른 점이 더 많은지 궁금해. 조부모님은 부부는 서로를 보완해야 한다고 말씀하셔. 어떤 면에서 나는 그분들의 의견에 동의해. 아빠는 약간 변덕스러워. 운전할 때 아빠는 무모한 운전자들 때문에 쉽게 화를 내셔. 그리고 나서 아빠는 속도를 높여서 그들을 겁주려고 하셔. 아빠는 심지어 그들이 틀렸다고 말로 확인해주고 싶어하셔. 엄마는 항상 아빠가 침착하시도록 설득하셔. 엄마는 아빠를 진정시키는 소질이 있어.

Exercise

A

1. spouse
2. appointment
3. outgoings
4. overdue
5. bond
6. complement
7. respect
8. temperamental
9. reckless
10. accelerate

B

1. soothing
2. 말로
3. 공포
4. contrast
5. tardily
6. 우물쭈물하는
7. prudent
8. complain

C

1. persuades
2. confirmation
3. respects
4. auto banking
5. Consequently
6. overdue
7. prudent
8. punctual

1. give a ride	태워주다
2. patriotic	애국적인
3. congested	정체된
4. strenuous	부단한
5. genre	장르
6. presidential	대통령의
7. contemporary	동시대의
8. pledge	공약, 서약
9. negative	부정적인
10. embassy	대사관
11. hypnosis	최면
12. money-oriented	금전만능의
13. renowned	유명한
14. philanthropist	박애주의자
15. passionate	열정적인
16. adventurer	모험가
17. leukemia	백혈병
18. subordinate	부하
19. famine	기아
20. assassinate	암살하다
21. subscribe	정기 구독하다
22. punctual	시간을 잘 지키는
23. biography	전기
24. tardy	늦은
25. fundamental	근본적인
26. acquaintance	아는 사람
27. formula	공식
28. accelerate	가속하다
29. relativity	상대성
30. temperamental	변덕스러운

Episode

사라에게.

사라, 너는 미술작품을 어떻게 감상하니? 우리 반은 미술관에 갔어. 로댕의 '생각하는 사람'이라는 조각상을 봤어. 로댕은 무엇을 표현하려고 했던 것일까? 무엇이 이 작품, '생각하는 사람'을 그의 걸작으로 만들었을까? 그는 사색하는 사람을 표현하고 싶었던 것일까? '생각하는 사람'은 불편한 듯 보였어. 내 짐작에는 '생각하는 사람'이 상처 입기 쉬운 사람을 상징하는 것 같아. 나는 그 조각상이 완벽한 비율인지 아닌지는 판단할 수 없어. 언젠가 나는 진흙으로 조그마한 작품을 만든 적이 있어. 전혀 대칭이맞지 않았어. 그 안에 균열도 많았어. 진흙에 수분이 충분하지 않았어. 나는 그 형편없는 작품을 완성하느라 며칠을 보내야 했어. 로댕은 자신의 위대한 작품을 끝내기 위해 틀림없이 왕성하게 작업했을 거야.

나중에 나는 몇몇 추상화 앞에 서게 되었어. 흠, 내가 그것들을 어떻게 평가할 수 있겠니? 나는 그것들의 저변에 깔린 의미를찾아내려고 애를 썼지만, 정말 애매했어. 어떤 그림들은 정말 이해하기가 어려웠어. 우리 선생님은 그것들이 우리의 잠재의식을 표현한 것이라고 하셨어. 내가 눈에 보이지 않는 것을 어떻게 파악할 수 있겠니? "이 그림들은 모호해"라고 혼잣말을 했어.

마지막으로, 나는 선명한 색채로 그려진 그림이 있는 곳으로 자리를 옮겼어. 그것들은 비교적 이해하기 쉬웠어. 그것들은 내게 구체적인 개념을 전달해줬어. 그것들은 이전 작품들과는 달랐어. 나는 그제서야 화가들과 상호 이해할 수가 있었어.

Exercise

A

1. vulnerable	2. crack
3. mold	4. gallery
5. concrete	6. subconscious
7. vague	8. evaluate
9. proportion	10. portray

B

1. appreciation	2. 조각품
3. 사색	4. symmetrical
5. completion	6. 보이지 않는
7. comprehend	8. 앞서다

C

1. masterpiece	2. uncomfortable
3. moisture	4. vigorously
5. abstract	6. ambiguous
7. vivid	8. mutual

Chapter 2 — Unit 6

Episode

다이어리에게.

우리 가족은 목초지로 가득한 한 농장을 방문했어. 그 목초지는 시골에 있었어. 우리가 도착했을 때, 한 무리의 소들이 풀밭에 있는 것을 보았어. 그리고 거기에는 가축들도 많았어.

"나는 양들이 풀 뜯어먹는 것을 지켜볼래"라고 후니가 말했어. 아마 우화가 생각난 모양이야. 우화에서 양은 늘 순수하고 반면에 늑대는 사악해. 또 다른 이야기들에서 양은 종종 단순해. 하지만 때로 온순한 사람에 비유되기도 해.

세리와 나는 우유를 짜내기 위해 소의 젖을 짰어. 그들의 눈을 보면서, 나는 일종의 친밀감을 느꼈어. 마치 내가 젖소와 동일시되는 기분이었어. 우리 사이에 텔레파시가 있는 것 같은 느낌이었어. 나는 소들의 생각을 직관으로 알 수 있을 것 같았어. 왜 우리가 인간에게 우유를 제공해줘야 하지? 왜 우리가 인간에게 이용되어야 하지? 그들을 섬겨야 할 운명인가? 우리는 오랫동안 농부들의 동무가 되어줬어. 그들은 우리를 귀하게 여겨야 해. 우리는 밭을 가는 데 이용되어 왔어. 추수하는 데에도 이용되어 왔어. 우리는 육체노동에 이용되어 왔어. 비참한 조건에서 살아왔어. 우리는 인간에게 일관되게 노동력을 주고 있어. 인간들이 농사를 성공적으로 짓는 데 우리가 필수적이라고 생각하지 않니? 소들이 나에게 자신들의 이야기를 해달라고 요구하는 것 같았어. 정말 묘한 기분이었어!

Exercise

A

1. extract	2. urge
3. identify	4. naive
5. meadow	6. harvest
7. fable	8. peasant
9. pastureland	10. exploit

B

1. innocent	2. intimate
3. 텔레파시의	4. intuit
5. 예정된	6. honorable
7. 일관되게	8. 악, 부패

C

1. rural	2. herd
3. livestock	4. meek
5. provide	6. harnessed
7. plowing	8. wretched

Chapter 2 — Unit 7

Episode

보미에게.

터키는 정말 찬란한 문화를 가지고 있어. 터키는 여러 가지가 통합된 곳이야. 그곳은 동양과 서양의 문화를 모두 경험할 수 있는 좋은 곳이야. 또한 그곳은 이슬람 문화의 영향을 받아왔어. 이슬람 문화는 터키에서 정말 융성했어. 터키 사람들은 종교적이야. 라마단 기간 동안 금식을 해. 그들은 하루에 다섯 번 기도해. 모스크가 많은데, 그곳은 교회처럼 성스러운 장소야. 모스크는 미적으로 아름다워. 모스크의 타일은 기하학 무늬를 보여줘.

보미, 너는 이슬람 문화에 대해 어떻게 생각하니? 이슬람 문화에 대해 편견을 가지고 있지는 않니? 여행 전에 나는 피상적인 지식밖에 없었어. 돼지고기가 금기라는 것 정도만 알고 있었어. 나는 그들의 문화를 간과했던 거야. 나는 이슬람교도들이 많은 무역로를 확립했다는 것을 몰랐어. 무역에 있어서 그들은 정말 개척자였어. 나는 많은 사람들이 그들의 웅장한 문화를 과소평가했다고 확신해.

그들의 문화 유산에 관한 정보가 정확하게 보여지지 않는다는 사실이 안타깝지 않니? 그들의 역사는 왜곡된 것 같아. 나는 영화와 TV 프로그램에서 충분한 정보를 주고 있지 않다는 것을 몰랐어. 예를 들어, 이슬람교도들은 종종 테러리스트로 묘사되잖아. 어떤 프로그램에서는 테러리스트들의 침략에 초점을 맞추기도 해. 아니면 아름다운 궁전이나 문화가 아니라 비위생적인 장소를 집중적으로 다루기도 해. 그런 것이 우리가 이슬람 문화에 대해 편견을 갖도록 유도하는 것은 아닐까?

내일 우리는 스페인으로 갈 거야. 우리는 유명한 이슬람 건축물인 알람브라를 가 볼 거야. 그곳은 아주 유명한 관광지 중 하나야. 너에게 사진 보내는 것 잊지 않을게.

Exercise

A

1. geometric	2. underestimate
3. taboo	4. biased
5. fast	6. legacy
7. invasion	8. pioneer
9. Western	10. superficial

B

1. splendid	2. 통합하다
3. 기도	4. aestheticism
5. 확립하다	6. accuracy
7. depict	8. 위생적인

C

1. flourished	2. religious
3. sacred	4. prejudices
5. majestic	6. distorted
7. insufficient	8. attractions

Episode

세리: 우리 집안 장식 좀 바꾸어볼까? 가구 위치를 좀 바꿔볼 수 있잖아. 내가 언니 방을 어떻게 다시 정리할 수 있는지 보여줄게. 벽지를 바꾸어 방을 좀 더 화사하게 할 수 있어.

보미: 너는 자신 있어 보이는구나. 하지만 나는 네 디자인 컨셉이 맘에 드는지 잘 모르겠다.

세리는 자신이 아주 예술감각이 있다고 생각한다. 자신이 다재다능하다고 믿는다. 공예품 만드는 것을 좋아한다. 세리는 한때 보석함을 만들어 상을 타기도 했다. 자기의 보석함이 정교하게 디자인 되었다고 말했다. 또한 자신의 보석함이 모든 소녀들을 사로잡았다고 했다. 그녀는 자신의 보석함이 선풍적이라고 생각했다. 나는 그녀가 디자이너로서 직업을 갖는 것을 쉽게 상상할 수 있다. 한 디자인 경시대회에서 그녀는 구슬을 단 일회용 반창고를 만들었다. 나는 그것이 정말 비실용적일 거라고 생각했다. 하지만 세리는 상당한 금액의 상금을 받을 것이라고 기대했다. 세리는 자기의 일회용 반창고가 두드러질 것이라고 말했다.

보미: 세리, 벽지 색깔은 뭐로 할 거야? 분홍색으로 할 거야?

세리: 정말 우연의 일치네! 어떻게 나와 같은 생각을 했어? 이 핑크색 천도 핑크 벽지와 잘 어울릴 거야.

세리: 하지만 우리가 색깔을 고르는 건 선택의 여지가 있어, 그렇지? 나는 네가 생각하는 색깔에 매우 회의적이야. 계획을 바꾸는 것이 어때?

그때 후니가 자신의 생각을 가지고 불쑥 끼어들었다. 그는 자신을 상징하는 파란색을 골랐다. 아마 그는 슈퍼맨에 대해 생각하고 있었던 것같다. 이봐, 세리와 후니. 우리 집안 장식을 바꾸는 것은 좀 뒤로 미루어야겠다.

Exercise

A

1. sensational
2. interject
3. bead
4. wallpaper
5. impractical
6. modify
7. decor
8. career
9. coincidence
10. craft

B

1. decorative
2. 예술적인
3. 다재다능한
4. 보석으로 장식한
5. perception
6. prominent
7. 회의론자
8. 상징하다

C

1. decorative
2. 예술적인
3. 다재다능한
4. 보석으로 장식한
5. perception
6. prominent
7. 회의론자
8. 상징하다

1. appreciate	감상하다, 평가하다
2. sculpture	조각품
3. vulnerable	상처입기 쉬운
4. symmetrical	대칭의
5. vigorously	원기 왕성하게
6. ambiguous	애매한
7. vague	모호한, 애매한
8. concrete	구체적인
9. pastureland	목초지
10. vicious	사악한
11. extract	뽑다, 추출물
12. intuit	직관으로 알다
13. plow	갈다, 쟁기
14. exploit	이용하다
15. consistently	일관되게
16. integrated	통합된
17. flourish	융성하다
18. prejudice	편견
19. overlook	간과하다
20. distort	왜곡하다
21. underestimate	과소평가하다
22. insufficient	불충분한
23. architecture	건축물
24. concept	개념
25. versatile	다재다능한
26. elaborately	정교하게
27. perceive	알아차리다
28. substantial	상당한
29. fabric	천, 헝겊
30. interject	끼어들다

Chapter 3 — Unit 9

Episode

다이어리에게,
후니의 행동으로 보아 나는 뭔가 잘못되었다고 추론했어.

보미: 왜 그래, 후니?
후니: 왜 여자아이들은 남자아이들에 대해 환상을 갖는 거야? 여자아이들 사이에 성차별이 그렇게 만연해 있는 줄 몰랐어. 왜 분수 같은 수학 문제는 남자아이들이 더 잘할 거라고 생각해? 여자아이들은 재활용통 같은 무거운 물건은 남자아이들이 날라야 한다고 생각해. 왜 남자아이들이 그것을 해야 해? 우리가 성차별의 피해자야. 이따금 여자아이들은 우리를 노예 취급해. 여자아이들은 무책임해. 그들은 그런 일이 자기들한테 아주 힘든 척하잖아.

후니가 이 문제에 그렇게 민감한 이유를 나는 알고 있어. 자신의 감정을 감추고 있어. 후니는 새로운 반 친구 태지가 여자아이들한테 더 인기가 있을까 봐 두려워하는 거야. 태지는 무술을 잘해. 태지가 학교에 전학 오기 전에는, 후니가 가장 인기 있는 남학생이었어. 그 자리를 내 주고 싶지 않은 거야. 그는 그 자리를 지키고 싶어해. 이제 그는 여자아이들의 태도를 차별 탓으로 돌리고 있어. 남자아이들은 가끔 자신들의 신체적 힘을 증명하기 위해 특정한 통과의례를 거쳐야 해. 남자아이들은 힘을 자신들이 가진 미덕이라고 생각하기 때문에 싸워. 그들은 약한 남자아이들은 자주 무시당한다고 생각해. 후니는 태지가 자기보다 더 남자다운 특징을 많이 가졌다고 생각하는 거야.
후니, 여자아이들은 커다란 근육이 아니라 따뜻한 가슴을 가진 남자아이들을 좋아하는 경향이 있어. 여자아이들은 따뜻한 마음을 가진 남자아이들을 좋아해. 나는 네가 이상적인 타입의 남자라고 생각해. 이제 그가 더욱 동요하고 있어. 나는 늘 여자아이들이 성차별의 피해자라고 생각했었어. 나는 아주 여성스러운 옷을 항상 입어야 된다고 생각했었어. 이제 보니 남자아이들과 여자아이들 모두가 성차별의 똑같은 피해자라는 걸 알겠어. 후니때문에 남자아이들도 사회적 압력을 느낀다는 것을 깨닫게 되었어.

Exercise

A

1. fraction
2. recycling
3. infer
4. feminine
5. virtue
6. exhausting
7. despise
8. attribute
9. inclined
10. issue

B

1. illusory
2. 널리 퍼진
3. 노예제도
4. concealment
5. security
6. 남성다움
7. 이상적으로
8. agitate

C

1. victims
2. irresponsible
3. martial arts
4. surrender
5. rites of passage
6. warm-hearted
7. sexism
8. social pressure

Chapter 3 — Unit 10

Episode

사라에게,
정치인들은 어떤 사람들이야? 의회에 들어가기 위한 요건은 무엇일까? 어떤 자격이 필요한 것일까? 정치인이 되고 싶은 사람들은 엄격한 면접을 받아야 해. 면접 중에 그들이 표리부동한 사람인지 세심하게 조사해야 해. 많은 정치인들은 공통적인 특성이 있어. 그들은 정중한 척해. 그들은 유권자들에게 자신들의 행동이 투명할 것이라고 약속을 해. 하지만 일단 당선되면 정책이 바뀌어. 최근에 몇몇 정치인들이 뇌물수수 스캔들에 연루되었어. 할아버지께서는 사람들이 그 후보자들에게 투표하지 말았어야 했다고 말씀하셨어. 그들의 부패한 행동은 아주 심각해. 나는 그들이 즉시 사임해야 한다고 생각해. 대법원이 언제 이 사건에 개입할까? 경찰은 그들을 철저하게 수사할까? 사이버 공간에서 우리는 정치인들을 재미있는 방법으로 조롱할 수 있어. 내 친구들은 그들에 관한 풍자적인 글을 웹페이지에 올리는 것을 좋아해. 이러한 것들이 유행병처럼 전국을 휩쓸고 있어. 그것들은 사람들이 부패한 정치인들을 어떻게 생각하는지 잘 보여줘. 이따금 최고위급 정부 관리들은 동물로 묘사돼. 그들은 종신형을 선고받아. 그들은 벌레처럼 기며 사죄를 해. 우리는 그들을 시야에서 사라지게 할 수도 있어. 너도 풍자 게임이나 조크에 관해 관심이 있으면 알려줘. 사라, 미국은 민주당과 공화당의 양당제라고 들었어. 어느 당이 장애인과 같은 소수 사람들의 권리를 더 지지하니? 양쪽 당 모두 인종주의에 강하게 반대하니? 나는 민주당은 더 진보적이고 공화당은 더 보수적이라고 들었어. 어쨌든, 두 당이 다 국민들을 위해 일했으면 해.

Exercise

A

1. transparent
2. bribery
3. conservative
4. trait
5. official
6. two-party system
7. policy
8. minority
9. epidemic
10. requirement

B

1. 엄격
2. 정중하게
3. corruptible
4. resign
5. satire
6. 설명하다
7. 인종
8. liberate

C

1. qualifications
2. two-faced
3. nominees
4. investigate
5. mock
6. crawl
7. vanish
8. life-long imprisonment

Episode

다이어리에게,
성범죄자에 대한 사라의 이야기는 끔찍했어. 어떻게 전자발찌를 평생 차고 살 수 있을까? 사람들이 쉽게 알아볼 텐데, 어떻게 다른 주민들과 어울릴 수 있을까? 그의 자존심은 어떻게 될까? 사람들이 쳐다볼 때마다 굴욕감을 느낄 텐데. 그러면 그는 새로운 동네 사람들과 동화될 수 없을 거야. 이런 처벌에는 찬반양론이 있어. 아주 논란이 되는 쟁점이야. 찬성론자들은 이 처벌이 효과적이라고 말해. 범죄율이 감소할 것이라고 주장해. 하지만 반대론자들은 이러한 형태의 처벌에 관해 우려를 나타내고 있어. 인권운동가들은 이러한 생각에 강력히 반대해.
이번 주 신문들은 유괴에 대한 기사로 가득해. 어린이 두 명이 납치된 후에 살해되어 발견되었어. 대부분의 사람들이 이것 때문에 공포에 떨게 되고, 그것이 논쟁을 유발시키고 있어. 사형제도에 대한 문제가 다시 불거지고 있어. 어떤 사람들은 국민의 안전이 우선이라고 주장해. 신문에서 사설 몇 개를 읽어보는데, 많은 언론인들이 이 문제에 관해 자신들의 견해를 표현했어. 나는 사형제도가 폐지되어야 한다고 생각해.
세리는 향수 대신 헤어 스프레이를 가지고 다녀. 세리는 누군가가 자신을 괴롭히려고 하면 그것을 사용할 것이라고 해. 스프레이분사가 그 사람의 행동을 막아줄 것이라고 믿고 있어. 세리는 남을 괴롭히는 사람들을 만났을 때 늘 용감했어. 세리는 누군가 자신을 위협해도 절대 타협하지 않았어. 세리는 자신의 생명은 지킬 만한 가치가 있으니까 자신을 지켜야 한다고 주장해.

Exercise

A

1. priority
2. controversial
3. harass
4. death penalty
5. defend
6. sex offender
7. editorial
8. journalist
9. assimilate
10. proponent

B

1. 전자공학
2. residential
3. 범인
4. opponent
5. provoke
6. 폐지하다
7. 직면하다
8. worthless

C

1. humiliated
2. pros and cons
3. kidnapping
4. murdered
5. panic
6. perfume
7. bullies
8. emission

Episode

다이어리에게,
후니와 그의 친구가 컴퓨터 게임을 하고 있어. 그들은 서로를 적이라고 불러. 각자는 자기 자신을 강력한 군대라고 불러. 각자 전략이 있어. 그들은 전함을 급파해. 그들은 군대도 파병해. 각각은 동맹국도 있어. 그들은 많은 공격용 무기를 사용해. 그들은 원자탄을 투하해 서로를 공격해. 그들은 서로의 영토를 점령하기 위해 애써. 그리고 승자는 상대를 몰아내는 사람이야. 마침내 "임무 완수"라는 메시지가 떠. 왜 남자아이들은 이런 폭력적인 게임을 좋아할까? 후니는 그것이 실제가 아니라 가상일 뿐이라고 말해. 최근에 중동에서 전쟁이 발발했어. 관계 당국들이 조약을 맺기 위해 만나고 있어. 그들은 언제 전쟁 종식을 선언할까? 가능성이 없는 것일까? 정전을 선언하는 것이 그렇게 어려울까? 정의를 위해 이 전쟁을 시작했다고 어떤 대통령이 말했어. 하지만 양 쪽 다 아직도 서로를 비난해. 선량한 사람들이 난민이 되어가고 있어. 그들은 의약품과 음식이 부족해. 모든 시설들이 파괴되었어. 그들은 기간시설이 파괴되었어. 어떤 사람들은 양쪽이 천연자원을 놓고 싸운다고 말해. 지도자들은 양심이 있을까? 그들은 심지어 분명하게 그들이 평화와 정의를 원한다고 말해. 우리가 어떻게 그들의 의중을 확인할 수 있을까? 나는 그들이 생명이 귀하다고 생각하는지가 의심스러워.

Exercise

A

1. displace
2. enemy
3. blame
4. territory
5. infrastructure
6. ally
7. demolish
8. treaty
9. declare
10. dispatch

B

1. mightiness
2. 전략을 짜다
3. occupied
4. 선교사, 전도의
5. 가능하게
6. justify
7. conscience
8. 확인할 수 있는

C

1. troops
2. assault
3. violent
4. broke out
5. cease-fire
6. refugees
7. resources
8. explicit

REVIEW TEST — Unit 9~ Unit 12

1. infer	추론하다
2. prevalent	널리 퍼진, 보급된
3. irresponsible	무책임한
4. conceal	숨기다, 은폐하다
5. despise	얕보다, 무시하다
6. inclined	~하고 싶어 하는
7. agitated	흥분된, 동요한
8. rigorous	엄격한
9. courteous	정중한
10. bribery	뇌물수수
11. corrupt	부패한, 타락시키다
12. mock	조롱하다
13. crawl	기다, 아첨하다
14. racism	인종차별주의
15. conservative	보수적인
16. self-esteem	자존심, 자부심
17. assimilate	동화되다
18. controversial	논쟁의
19. panic	공황, 허둥대는
20. abolish	폐지하다
21. confront	직면하다
22. mighty	강력한
23. troop	군대
24. violent	폭력적인
25. imaginary	상상의, 가상의
26. treaty	조약
27. declare	선언하다
28. lack	부족하다, 결핍
29. conscience	양심
30. term	용어

Chapter 4 — Unit 13

Episode

다이어리에게,

세계 시장이 안정적이지 못한 것 같아. 그렇다면 디플레이션은 뭐지? 신문에 의하면 실업률은 계속해서 높아지고 있어. 기업가들은 직원들을 많이 고용할 수가 없어. 어떤 직원들은 정리해고 당하고 있어. 회사들은 자금난을 겪고 있다고 말해. 그들을 돕기 위해 정부에게 법을 개정하도록 요구하면 어떨까? 그러면 은행들은 그것에 따라야 할 거야. 내 말은, 은행은 그냥 우리 모두를 위해 현금을 충분히 찍어내면 돼. 그러나 어떤 경제학자들은 그것이 인플레이션만 유발시킬 것이라고 말해. 요즈음 농부들이 시내에서 집회를 하고 있어. 그들은 심지어 자신들의 농산물을 태워버리기도 했어. 그들은 왜 항의하는 것일까? 자신들의 반정부 감정을 표출하는 걸까? 농부들은 자신들이 세계화의 피해자라고 주장해. 그들은 국산품이 수입상품의 낮은 가격 때문에 수입상품과 경쟁할 수 없다고 주장해. 정부가 자신들을 도와줄 조치를 취해줄 것을 요구해. 우리가 수입품에 무거운 관세를 붙인다면 어떨까? 내 말은 무거운 수입관세 부과 말야. 유가도 치솟았어. 이런 오름세 물가가 소비자 지출을 억제해. 오름세 물가는 시장을 크게 침체시킬 거야. 아빠는 출퇴근할 때 지하철을 이용하셔야 할 거야. 상품들의 가격도 오르고 있어. 엄마는 우리가 절약해야 한다고 하셔. 엄마는 내 용돈도 깎을 작정이야.

엄마: 보미, 대통령이 TV에 나와서 이 역경을 극복하려면 열심히 일해야 한대.

보미: 엄마, 엄마의 계획이 적절하다고 생각해요? 내가 파산하면 어떻게 돼요? 난 빚지고 싶지 않아요.

Exercise

A

1. protest	2. rally
3. deflation	4. restrain
5. recession	6. comply
7. adequate	8. imported
9. financial	10. soar

B

1. unemployed	2. 개정하다
3. agricultural	4. 풍부하다
5. globalize	6. 억제하다
7. 절약	8. bankruptcy

C

1. stable	2. laid off
3. inflation	4. sentiment
5. take some measures	6. imposing
7. commute	8. intends

Episode

다이어리에게,

아빠, 오늘 주가지수 어때요? "이 품목이 가치가 저평가된 것 같아요"라고 후니가 말해. 그는 한 전문가의 설명을 인용하고 있을 뿐이야. 후니는 경제캠프에서 수료증을 받았어. 그는 그 코스를 우등으로 수료했다고 자랑하고 있어. 그는 자신의 수료증을 정말 소중히 간직하고 있어. "이 그래프는 뭐야?"라고 후니에게 물었어. 아마도 그는 경제학의 몇몇 기본원리를 생각해내려고 하는 것 같아. 그는 자원은 제한되어 있는데 인간의 욕망은 끝이 없다는 말을 계속해서 해. 후니는 마치 학자처럼 말하고 있어. 그는 경제학에 대해 심오한 지식을 얻은 척해. 그는 또한 금융 분석가인 척하기를 정말 좋아해.

후니: 아빠, 만화영화는 잘 나가는 업종인가요? 저는 캠프에서 어떤 업종의 성공 가능성이 중요하다는 것을 배웠어요. 그리고 우리 화재 보험 들었어요?

아빠: 아니, 하지만 자동차 보험은 있단다.

후니: 아빠, 새로 산 컴퓨터 CD의 품질보증서 어디 있어요?

아빠: 아마 서랍에 있을 거야.

보미: 후니, 내 투자 계획 좀 도와줄래?

후니: 물론. 은행에 더 많은 돈을 예치하지 그래? 아니면 부동산에 투자하는 게 어때?

내 은행 계좌에 대략 5만원 정도 있어. 약 20원 정도의 이자가 붙었어. 만일 이 정도로 이자가 붙으면, 나는 언제쯤 돈을 모아서 백만장자가 될 수 있을까?

Exercise

A

1. presumably
2. cherish
3. analyst
4. millionaire
5. stock index
6. interest
7. graph
8. insured
9. with honors
10. scholar

B

1. quotation
2. 저평가된
3. 추정하다
4. infinite
5. prospective
6. 투자자
7. 축적
8. prosperous

C

1. certificate
2. undervalued
3. finite
4. profound
5. warranty
6. insurance
7. deposit
8. real estate

Episode

사라에게,

사라, 서울 수도권에 몇 명이나 산다고 생각하니? 우리 사회학 선생님이 그러시는데 전체 인구의 4분의 1이 이 지역에 산대. 많은 사람들이 시골에서 여기로 이주한다는 것도 배웠어. 이젠 왜 아빠가 지하철이 만원이라고 불평하시는지 이해할 수 있어. 아빠는 서울에서의 삶의 질에 만족하지 못하셔. 은퇴하면 서울을 떠나시겠다고 가끔 말씀하셔. 외딴 곳에 땅을 조금 사시겠대. 식물학자처럼 아빠는 식물을 재배하는 방법에 관한 책을 읽으셔. 아빠는 유기농 과일 재배에 관한 책을 읽으셨어. 그리고 지금은 포도나무 이식하는 방법에 관해 읽고 계셔. 나는 아빠가 어느 포도가 익었는지 구별하실지 모르겠어. 수확을 늘리기 위해 무엇을 해야 할지 아실까? 엄마가 농사에 적응하실까?

보미: 네가 카이트랑 놀던 빈터가 어디니?

후니: 없어졌어. 지금은 공사 부지가 되어버렸어.

건설이 번창하는 업종인 것은 분명하다. 그것은 성황 중이다. 우리 동네 청사진이 빠르게 바뀌고 있다. 대부분의 낡은 집이 현대식 건물로 바뀌었다. 아파트가 계속 늘어나고 있다. 그것은 마치 새로운 건물들이 주변의 모습을 바꾸면서 계속 복제되는 것만 같다. 우리 동네는 사라가 떠난 후로 많이 달라졌다. 후니와 카이트는 빈터에서 놀곤 했다. 이제 그곳은 건설 근로자 외에는 출입 금지이다. 우리 엄마는 땅값이 오르기를 기대하신다. 하지만 후니와 카이트는 놀이터를 그리워한다.

Exercise

A

1. booming
2. overcrowded
3. thriving
4. restricted
5. organic
6. replicate
7. transplant
8. modernized
9. migrate
10. acre

B

1. metropolitan
2. dwelling
3. 식물학
4. 익다, 익히다
5. adaptability
6. vacancy
7. 달라지다
8. multiply

C

1. quality
2. retirement
3. discern
4. yield
5. construction
6. blueprint
7. transforming
8. land price

REVIEW TEST Unit 13~ Unit 15

1. stable	안정된
2. lay off	정리해고하다
3. amendment	개정, 수정
4. comply	따르다
5. rally	집회, 규합하다
6. imported	수입된
7. impose	부과하다
8. soar	치솟다
9. commodity	상품
10. adequate	적절한, 충분한
11. quote	인용하다, 인용문
12. certificate	수료증, 증명하다
13. cherish	소중히 여기다
14. finite	제한된
15. profound	심오한
16. prosperous	성공한
17. warranty	품질보증서
18. insurance	보험
19. approximately	대략
20. deposit	예치하다, 예치
21. dwell	거주하다
22. migrate	이주하다
23. discern	구별하다
24. ripe	익은
25. yield	수확, 산출하다
26. adapt	적응하다
27. thriving	번창하는, 성공하는
28. modernized	현대화된
29. multiply	늘다, 증가하다
30. transform	변형시키다

Chapter 5 Unit 16

Episode

다이어리에게,
첨단기술 제품은 다양한 방법으로 적용될 수 있어. 우리의 새로운 기술 덕분에, 장소와 시간은 더 이상 장애가 되지 않아. 새로운 기술은 우리의 생활에 엄청난 변화를 가져왔어. 우리는 새로운 기술 덕분에 과거에는 상상할 수 없었던 것들을 경험할 수 있어. 우리 아빠는 국제 회의를 하기 위해 해외로 가실 필요가 없어. 아빠는 전통적인 방법으로 회의를 하는 대신에 일주일에 한 번 화상 회의를 하셔. 어느 때든지 세계 어디에 있는 고객들과도 이야기를 할 수 있어. 만약 우리 조상들이 살아온다면, 그들은 우리의 기술을 혁신적인 것이라고 부를 거야.

다이어리, 우리 엄마는 절대로 첨단 기술을 빨리 받아들이는 분이 아니셔. 디지털 시계보다는 아날로그 시계를 더 좋아하셔. 몇 달 전에 엄마는 인터넷뱅킹 서비스를 사용하지 않으셨어.
엄마는 제대로 되지 않을 것이라고 걱정하셨던 거야. 그렇지만 공공요금을 인터넷뱅킹으로 지불하신 후에는, 그것이 얼마나 간편한지 알게 되셨어. 요즘 엄마는 매달 내 용돈을 내 은행 계좌로 송금하셔. 엄마는 인터넷으로 우리 조부모님께 사진도 전송하셔.

사라는 흥미로운 박물관에 대해 나에게 이메일을 보냈어. 만일 미술 작품을 만지면, 즉시 상호작용이 가능한 작품으로 변해. 사라가 그림을 만졌을 때, 그림 속의 피사체가 춤을 추고 사라의 질문에 대답도 했어. 예를 들면, 레오나르도 다빈치의 모나리자가 15세기의 귀족들의 삶에 대해 설명했어. 모나리자는 그들의 독특한 풍습에 대해서도 설명했어. 그녀는 또한 초상화를 그리는 것이 그 시대의 유행이었다고 말했어.

다이어리, 집 한 채 크기만한 거대한 10달러짜리 지폐를 상상할 수 있니? 이상하게 들리지 않니? 하지만 100배 확대된 10달러짜리의 견본을 상상해 봐. 사라가 그 지폐의 일부분에 손을 댔을 때 그것은 입체적이 되었어. 흥미롭게도 화면에 심판이 나타나서 그녀에게 공을 던졌어. 나는 이 시스템을 누가 생각해냈는지 궁금해. 그 그래픽은 정말 놀라워.

Exercise

A

1. analog watch	2. utility
3. subject	4. inconceivable
5. specimen	6. interactive
7. weird	8. barrier
9. referee	10. revolutionary

B

1. 엄청난	2. convention
3. adopt	4. 전송
5. 귀족정치	6. uniqueness
7. portrayal	8. 상상할 수 있는

C

1. conferences	2. clients
3. Internet banking	4. malfunction
5. transmits	6. converted
7. three-dimensional	8. devised

Episode

다이어리에게.

블로그를 하는 것은 나의 창의적인 아이디어를 표현하는 수단이야. 몇 주 동안 나는 내 블로그의 음악과 사진을 업데이트했어. 나는 음악과 볼케이노의 사진을 다운로드했어. 그리고 나서 나는 음악과 사진이라는 두 구성요소의 짝을 맞추었어. 가끔 나는 고전 음악과 그에 어울리는 볼케이노의 사진을 맞추었어. 나는 최고의 쌍을 결합시키는 데 몇 시간이 걸렸어. 결과는 놀랄 만한 것이었어. 매일 400명 이상의 사람들이 나의 블로그를 방문했어. 그들은 꽤 긍정적이고 칭찬하는 메시지를 남겼어. 어떤 사람은 내가 사용한 자료들이 독창적이라고 썼어. 나는 메시지를 읽는 것이 즐거웠어. 다른 사람들을 즐겁게 하는 것이 만족스러웠어. 오늘 난 경고 메시지를 발견했어. 어떤 음악 파일은 삭제되어 있었어. 나는 매우 혼란스러웠어. 메시지에는 "당신은 이 자료를 사용할 수 없습니다"라고 쓰여 있었어.

보미: 뭐가 잘못됐나요? 제가 사이버 경찰에게 체포될까요? 제 자료에 뭔가 결함이 있나요? 엄마. 왜 그 사람들은 제 자료가 불법이라고 생각할까요?

엄마: 그건 저작권법에 관련된 거야.

보미: 하지만 저는 그 자료들을 제 개인적인 관심 이외의 다른 용도로는 사용하지 않았어요.

엄마: 다른 사람들의 창작물은 개인적인 재산으로 취급되어야 해. 네가 자료를 주인의 허가 없이 사용했다면, 그건 절도와 같은거야. 만약 누군가가 자신의 자료에 관해 저작권을 주장한다면, 너는 그걸 그들에게 돌려주어야 해. 자료의 주인은 돈을 받으려고 너를 고소하려고 할지도 몰라.

보미: 저는 제가 저작권을 침해한 줄 몰랐어요. 지금부터는 다른 사람의 자료를 사용하기 전에 동의를 얻을 거예요.

Exercise

A

1. component
2. outlet
3. infringe
4. cybercop
5. warn
6. copyright
7. assert
8. delete
9. download
10. blog

B

1. combination
2. 현상
3. 독창성
4. 유쾌한
5. defective
6. illegal
7. 사용하다
8. consenter

C

1. updated
2. classical
3. positive
4. gratifying
5. materials
6. defects
7. property
8. sue

Episode

아빠: 여권을 갱신해야겠다.

보미: 기간을 연장한다고 하셨잖아요.

아빠: 새 여권이 더 안전할 거야. 위조를 방지하려고 홀로그램 같은 최첨단 기술이 사용되기 때문이야.

아빠는 위조품이 발견되었다는 뉴스가 나간 바로 후에 이렇게 말씀하셨다.

한국 휴대 전화는 인기가 있다. 어떤 나라에서는 그 제품들이 시장을 거의 독점하고 있다. 오늘 우리는 가짜 휴대 전화에 관한 뉴스를 보았다. 분명히 이 휴대 전화의 로고와 디자인은 한국 휴대 전화에 있는 것과 똑같다. 소비자들은 속아서 자신들이 진짜 제품을 구입한다고 믿을 수도 있다. 어떻게 이런 일이 일어난 것일까?

슬프게도 몇몇 한국인들이 이런 일로 또한 고소되었다. 그들은 이 문제에 깊이 연루되어 있다고 한다. 주장에 따르면, 그들은 외국의 사업가들과 공모했다. 그들은 이것에 대한 대가로 돈을 받기를 기대했을 것이다. 그러나 한국 회사의 재정적 손실은 헤아릴 수 없다. 만일 이 반역자들이 유죄로 밝혀지면, 그들은 그 회사의 손실에 대해 보상을 해야 할 것이다. 나는 한국 제품의 완전함에 흠이 갈까 걱정이다. 만일 한국 제품에 대한 사람들의 생각이 안 좋아지면 어떻게 하지?

보미: 그것이 외교 논쟁으로 이어질 수 있나요?

아빠: 그렇지. 그것은 관련된 나라 간에 적개심을 불러일으킬 수도 있어. 위조법은 실행되어야 해.

보미: 그 법은 강화되어야겠어요. 저는 가짜 상품이 그렇게 많은 문제를 야기하는지 몰랐어요.

Exercise

A

1. accuse
2. compensate
3. cutting-edge
4. monopolize
5. immeasurable
6. traitor
7. dispute
8. renew
9. enforce
10. trick

B

1. 광범위한
2. forger
3. evidence
4. 주장하다
5. 공모하다
6. compensation
7. diplomat
8. hostility

C

1. passports
2. implemented
3. fake
4. genuine
5. in return for
6. integrity
7. tarnished
8. reinforced

Unit 16~ Unit 18

1. high-tech	첨단 기술의
2. drastic	엄청난, 격렬한
3. revolutionary	혁신적인
4. malfunction	고장, 고장나다
5. interactive	상호작용을 하는
6. aristocrat	귀족
7. weird	이상한
8. specimen	견본
9. devise	고안하다, 발명하다
10. subject	대상, 피사체
11. outlet	표현 수단, 배출구
12. phenomenal	놀랄 만한
13. complimentary	무료의, 칭찬하는
14. ingenious	독창적인
15. gratifying	만족스러운
16. material	자료
17. illegal	불법의
18. utilize	사용하다
19. theft	절도
20. infringe	침해하다
21. implement	이행하다
22. forgery	위조품, 위조
23. monopolize	독점하다
24. fake	가짜의, 모조품
25. genuine	진짜의
26. conspire	음모를 꾸미다
27. compensate	보상하다
28. tarnish	더럽히다, 흠
29. dispute	논쟁, 논쟁하다
30. reinforce	강화하다

Unit 19

Episode

다이어리에게,

어제 우리 가족은 놀라운 현상을 보았어. 전체 월식이었어. 지구, 태양과 달이 모두 일직선으로 정렬되었어. 하늘에서 일어나는 이런 종류의 현상은 자주 일어나지 않아. 그것을 관찰하는 동안, 후니는 외계에 있는 다른 행성을 탐험하고 싶다고 말했어. 그는 외계인들과 의사소통하는 것이 재미있을 거라고 생각했어. 세리는 후니에게 "우리가 외계인이 아이들을 유괴할 거라고 생각했던 것 기억하니?"라고 물었어. 후니와 세리는 외계인이라는 이름을 붙인 그들만의 게임을 만들었어. 그들은 그들의 팀을 화성에서 온 탐험대라고 이름붙였어. 그들은 화성인인 양했어.

게임에서 그들은 태양계를 탐험하는 외계인이었어. 그들은 후니의 로케트를 사용했고 그것을 인공위성이라고 불렀어. 게임에서 인공위성은 태양계를 궤도를 그리며 돌고 있었어. 그들은 여러 개의 공을 운석이라고 불렀어. 그들은 서로에게 공을 던져서 지구가 운석과 충돌하게 했어. 그들은 그 사건을 최후의 심판일이라고 불렀어. 만일 최후의 심판일이 온다면, 지구에 사는 모든 사람들은 위험에 처하겠지. 그것은 매우 엄청난 재앙일 거야.

나중에 우리는 천문학에 관한 책을 읽었어. 그 책에는 천문학적으로 중요한 사건이 연대순으로 설명되어 있었어. 그 책은 지난 수십 년간 일어난 사건에 대해서 설명하고 있었어. 그것들 중에서 1986년에 우주선이 폭발한 것이 가장 충격적이었어. 우주로 쏘아올려진 동물에 관해 읽는 것은 재미있었어. 우리는 중력이 거의 없는 우주에서 동물들에게 그 일이 있어났는지에 대해 얘기했어.

우리는 동물들의 그림을 보았는데 머리가 가끔 부풀어 올라 있었어. 책에 의하면, 그것은 우주에서 피가 머리로 몰리기 때문이야. 우리는 은하계 전체를 탐사하는 것이 가능한지 궁금했어. 후니는 우리가 우주 탐사선을 보내서 은하계 전체를 탐사할 수 있다고 생각했어. 후니, 너는 중요한 사실 하나를 빠뜨렸어. 이 우주는 광대해.

Exercise

A

1. solar system	2. chronological
3. outer space	4. gravity
5. orbit	6. launch
7. Extra-Terrestrials	8. space probe
9. doomsday	10. alien

B

1. exploration	2. 유괴하다
3. alignment	4. collision
5. 큰 재앙	6. astronomically
7. explosion	8. 은하계의

C

1. eclipse	2. celestial
3. Expedition	4. artificial satellite
5. meteorites	6. jeopardy
7. swollen	8. omitting

Episode

다이어리에게.

가끔 우리는 자연이 존재하는 것을 당연하게 생각하고 그것이 얼마나 중요한지 깨닫지 못해. 우리는 종종 자연을 오용하며 자연을 경제적 가치로만 계산해. 우리 학교는 식목일에 특별 행사를 열었어. 모든 학생들은 황사 때문에 마스크를 쓰고 있었어. 우리 학교 교장 선생님은 나무를 심으면서 그 행사를 개회하셨어. 나무를 심고 나서, 교장 선생님은 황사의 오염물질이 우리에게 주는 영향에 대해 말씀하셨어. 그는 우리 한반도에서 황사가 왜 증가했는지 설명하셨어. 그는 우리에게 무엇이 토양의 침식을 일으키는지 물으셨어. 그는 또한 산사태와 홍수의 원인을 묻기도 하셨어. 우리는 만장일치로 "삼림 벌채"라고 대답했어. 그는 우리가 환경을 돌보는 데 주의해야 한다고 다시 강조했어. 또한 "우리가 자연을 보존하지 않으면, 그것이 인간을 역습할 것입니다"라고 덧붙이셨어. 행사를 마치고 나서, 우리 반은 테마파크로 갔어. 그곳은 인기 있는 친환경 공원이었어. 거기에는 많은 종류의 식물들과 동물들이 있었어. 토끼와 같은 동물들은 집단으로 서식하고 있었어. 우리 선생님은 이 지역이 쓰레기 매립지였다고 말씀하셨어. 쓰레기는 어디로 갔지? 그것은 설명이 안될 것 같았어. 식물들은 도대체 어떻게 오염된 토양에서 자랐을까? 토양은 틀림없이 독성이 있을 거야. 사실, 엄청난 노력 덕분에 토양의 독성이 성공적으로 중화되었어. 중화시키려는 노력 덕분에 척박한 땅이 공원이 되었어. 경관은 완전히 바뀌었어. 몇몇 멸종 위기의 동식물들은 지금은 그곳에서 살 수 있어. 그것은 그들의 서식지가 복구되었다는 것을 의미해. 그곳에서 그들은 멸종되지 않을 거야. 테마파크의 환경 보호 노력을 보는 것이 매우 즐거웠어.

Exercise

A

1. flood	2. landfill
3. inaugurate	4. species
5. landscape	6. peninsula
7. barren	8. deforestation
9. habitat	10. Arbor Day

B

1. pollution	2. 계산하다
3. 조심	4. erode
5. contaminated	6. 독소
7. 중성의	8. extinct

C

1. take for granted	2. yellow dust
3. counterattack	4. landslides
5. eco-friendly	6. unaccountable
7. endangered species	8. colonies

Episode

다이어리에게.

경제 발전과 자연은 양립할 수 없는 것일까? 뉴스 보도에 따르면 우리는 이산화탄소 배출량을 줄여야 해. 많은 나라들은 자연 보호가 경제 발전보다 바람직하다고 인정해. 휘발유를 연료로 하는 대형 세단은 인기가 있었어. 요즘은 소형 하이브리드 자동차가 세단의 대안으로 등장하고 있어. 회사들은 화석 연료 대신 바이오 연료를 찾아야 할 거야. 그들은 압박감을 느낄지도 몰라. 그러나 사람들은 절제라는 교훈을 배우고 있어.

최근에 세리와 나는 몇몇 나라의 식량 위기에 대해 이야기했어. 세리는 유전자 조작 식품을 지지했었고, 그것이 답이 될 수 있다고 믿었어. 그러나 TV 환경 채널에 자주 노출되자 그녀의 생각이 변했어. 그녀는 면 재배지에 있는 염소를 특집으로 한 프로그램을 본 적이 있어. 염소는 유전적으로 조작된 목화를 먹었어. 목화를 장기간 섭취한 후, 어떤 염소는 기형적인 다리를 가지고 태어났어. 그 프로그램을 본 후, 지금 그녀는 유전자 조작 식품이 유해하다고 굳게 믿고 있어. 그녀는 건강에 신경쓰기 때문에 유전자 조작 제품은 먹지 않으려고 해.

세리는 소형 체리 토마토 밭을 가지고 있어. 그녀는 식물을 잘 키우지 못해. 세리는 어떤 동기로 자신의 밭을 만들었을까? 그녀는 가족들이 먹다 남긴 음식을 사용하는 방법을 찾으려고 노력했었어. 그녀는 남은 음식을 버리지 않기로 결심했어. 대신 그녀는 밭을 만들어서 그것을 비료로 사용하기로 했어. 세리는 분해된 음식이 토양을 더 비옥하게 만든다는 것을 배웠어. 그녀의 밭은 작은 생태계야. 환경주의자로서, 세리는 종종 나에게 "일회용 물품은 더 이상 사용하지 마"라고 말해. 그녀 덕분에 나는 종이컵과 비닐백을 사용하지 않으려고 해.

Exercise

A

1. genetically modified food	2. moderation
3. leftover	4. hybrid car
5. deformed	6. health-conscious
7. preservation	8. firmly
9. disposable	10. crisis

B

1. reduction	2. 비상사태
3. 압박하는	4. 노출
5. 연장된	6. motive
7. fertilize	8. decomposition

C

1. incompatible	2. powered
3. fossil fuels	4. plantation
5. cotton	
6. have a green thumb	
7. discard	8. eco-system

Chapter 6 — Unit 22

REVIEW TEST — Unit 19~ Unit 22

Episode

사라가 나에게 이메일을 보냈다.

보미에게,
엘니뇨는 거대한 허리케인을 일으켜서 남부 해안을 따라 위치한 마을들을 강타했어. 주민들은 그 지역에서 떠나라는 이야기를 들었어. 그럼에도 불구하고, 몇몇 사람들은 생명을 걸고 집에 남아 있기를 주장했어. 거대한 파도와 엄청난 급류가 마을 전체를 쓸어버렸어. 대부분의 마을 사람들은 집을 잃었어. 그들의 집과 마을은 완전히 파괴되었어. 파괴의 힘은 무시무시했어. 그것은 핵폭탄의 위력과 비교될 수 있었어. 희생자들은 음식, 옷, 대피소가 부족한 문제에 당면하게 되었어. 방송에서는 우리들에게 그들의 괴로워하는 얼굴을 보여주었어. 피해의 범위는 계속 넓어지고 있어. 정부는 그곳을 재해 지역으로 선포했어. 며칠 후에 허리케인의 힘은 약화되었어. 돌아온 주민들은 지쳐서 한숨을 내쉬었어. 집과 재산의 흔적은 거의 찾아볼 수 없었어. 전국적인 기부 물품들이 모아졌어. 음식과 약품이 인도주의 단체에 의해 배포되었어. 광범위한 소독이 전 지역에 걸쳐 행해졌어. 행정 당국에서는 전염병이 발생하지 않도록 노력하고 있어. 주민들은 끓인 물만 마시도록 권고받았어. 이제 정부는 마을 사람들에게 사회복지 혜택을 줄 거야. 그들은 사회적 불안을 예방하기 위해서 주민들이 집을 가능한 한 빨리 다시 지을 수 있도록 도울 거야.

Exercise

A

1. devastate
2. rebuild
3. nuclear bomb
4. proclaim
5. humanitarian
6. torrent
7. unrest
8. trace
9. risk
10. plague

B

1. 피난자
2. immensely
3. 부족함
4. 고통
5. weariness
6. 감소하는
7. 살균한
8. boiled

C

1. Nevertheless
2. homeless
3. formidable
4. extent
5. Nationwide
6. welfare
7. shelter
8. evacuate

1. align	정렬시키다	
2. abduct	유괴하다	
3. expedition	탐험대	
4. orbit	궤도를 그리며 돌다	
5. jeopardy	위험	
6. catastrophic	큰 재앙의	
7. swell	부풀다, 팽창하다	
8. omit	생략하다, 빠트리다	
9. calculate	계산하다, 평가하다	
10. inaugurate	~식을 행하다	
11. erosion	침식	
12. vigilant	주의하는	
13. unaccountable	설명할 수 없는	
14. contaminated	오염된	
15. barren	불모의	
16. extinct	멸종된	
17. incompatible	양립할 수 없는	
18. emerge	나타나다	
19. oppress	압박하다	
20. plantation	재배지	
21. deformed	기형의	
22. miniature	소형의, 축소모형	
23. fertilizer	비료	
24. decomposed	분해된	
25. immense	거대한	
26. formidable	무시무시한	
27. agonized	괴로워하는	
28. dwindle	감소하다	
29. proclaim	선언하다	
30. sterilize	소독하다	

EDGE